The Antireligious Views of Jesus as Expressed in His Parables

Scott Allen Medhaug

PublishAmerica
Baltimore

Hardcover 978-1-4512-3488-6
Softcover 978-1-4512-3489-3
PUBLISHED BY PUBLISHAMERICA, LLLP
www.publishamerica.com
Baltimore

Printed in the United States of America

I dedicate this book to my wonderful beautiful daughters; Mary Jessie (MJ) and Grace Elizabeth (Gracie). They were a gift from God and have lightened my life more than anything or anyone on earth. I wrote this book so they will have a part of me and know what I believed. There is nothing special about this book. It is simply my thoughts and feelings about the Christian religion today.

An unorthodox way of looking at Jesus' sayings

by Scott Allen Medhaug

Revised and edited by Lyle & Joyce Stout

PREFACE

Many topics have been repeated, but hopefully each time with different ways of explaining the topic in order to make the thoughts more understandable. I have cited thoughts that others have written and ideas that others have taught me in order to show that I agree with their comments or that the concept didn't come originally from me. Titles, along with other things, may be italicized for reasons that should be obvious.

Those eschatological colporteurs claiming their books are what will happen in the end of days or that they are inspired by God are no better than those that lead others away with their own words or deceptive miracles. This book claims no inspiration from God, and is only my thoughts and feelings about the human condition. The condemnation of such authors that claim some insight from God is latent in this writing.

The meanings of the parables are simple and I have used the parables to show that there is something wrong with the way we interpret the Bible. Because of religious traditions, we have accepted ideas that are non-Christian. These wrong concepts have been picked up by many cults in order to brainwash others into leaving a relationship with Christ and accepting such an organization as being the only one that represents

God. But a careful understanding of the antireligious tone of the Christian writings reveals the truth of what these cultish people are looking for; and that is self-centeredness. The parables of Jesus encapsulate the core of the meaning of the Gospels. By understanding the parables you will come to know what is needed in the Christian life. Most parables are Jesus' explanation of the functional church.

The first eight chapters of this book each deal with either a single parable, or multiple parables, with the intent of expressing the meaning of each parable relative to today. Each idea presented should be able to reflect back on the specific parable being examined. It may seem as though I have written little about some of the parables, but the content of the chapter should make the parable more thought provoking. The parables are important because within them you find the heart of the Gospel.

In the eighth and ninth chapters you will find smaller parables that I refer to as sayings. I do this because they are short stories that give a powerful point and can also help to understand larger stories told by Jesus. I am sure there were many of Jesus' stories that were not saved for us, but this does not mean that anything that God wanted us to know has been lost.

In part of the ninth chapter I deal with the parables in the Gospel of John as this is a book that is not well understood by Christians today. The whole of the writing of John is against Gnosticism and uses Gnostic concepts, with the intention of bringing a Gnostic believer back into orthodox beliefs. It is almost impossible to understand the deep concepts of this Gospel without understanding what Gnostics believed and how they lived. With just the three Parables in John's Gospel examined, you could easily write a whole book that would help many Christians to understand the concept of the Church and why Christian organizations are filled with both wheat and tares. This concept is important, for unlike the tares that are plants, the "tares" of the parable (which represent us) can change.

Contents

CHAPTER 3

CHAPTER 4

CHAPTER 5

CHAPTER 6

CHAPTER 10

CHAPTER 1
THE LANDOWNER

But they will reply, "It's no use. We will continue with our own plans; each of us will follow the stubbornness of his evil heart."

Jeremiah 18:12 (The Bible—New International Version)

Despair is the limit. Here are met the cowardly timorous ill-temper of self-love, and the proud defiant presumption of the mind—here they are met in equal importance.

Kierkegaard (Purity of Heart)

Truth is the cry of all, but the game of few
George Berkeley (Siris)

JESUS AND THE PHARISEES

The Pharisees latently seemed to comprehend Jesus' parables, as their anger was a reaction to the many stories that portrayed them negatively; however, in spite of the evidence, these religious leaders refused to admit that Jesus was the Messiah and thereby lost the positions they had acquired through their teachings. While they were trying to tempt him, Jesus turned the tables on the Pharisees by telling parables and asking questions. The Pharisees knew that they should not answer his questions, for the Pharisees and other religious leaders would thereby condemn themselves and contradict their own belief systems. Yet, the Pharisees' pride forced them to answer Jesus' questions, even while trying to hide their confusion. They understood Jesus' implications, but they could not embrace him because they wanted a Messiah that would lead them to a more powerful leadership position by overthrowing the established forces. They taught a concept of a political Messiah and consequently any references to suffering in the Bible they saw as referring to their nation. This political concept is still alive today in Israel and also manifests itself in many of the other religions in the world. Jesus' political time had not yet come and this made it difficult for Judaism to accept him as the Messiah at that time.

When looking at the problems between Jesus and the religious leaders, we should not believe the situation in anyway degrades the Jews. Ungodly individuals have fabricated an anti-Semitic view by exploiting the contentions between Jesus and the religious leaders, and for anyone that internalizes such belief, they will have a shallow understanding of what the gospel writers where trying to convey. This shallow view teaches something far removed from the didactic spirit of the Gospels.

We can and should understand Jesus' contemporary religious leaders as an example of religious leaders throughout history. We all are born into a society, and we grow to identify social norms as normal behaviors. Others social norms seem strange to us, even as our norms seem strange to other societies. Some have used this way of understanding to promote a concept of relativity, but that interjection provides another misconception of social norms. Social relativity suggests that nothing is right or wrong and therefore every act is purely situational. Furthermore, social relativity stands as not only weak, but also a tainted understanding of society. Underlining any social relativity construct, the concrete must also emerge. Accordingly, we can find something concrete about the way all religious leaders act when following their own gain. We learn about this attitude in Jesus' contemporary religious leaders as well as in many modern religious leaders. This problem emerges in many religious leaders today despite the Biblical teachings, as they follow in the same corrupt path as the Pharisees. It was the religious leaders that constrained the Jewish people from following Jesus, although they did so with little success. In fact, many Pharisees themselves eventually followed.

"Many things are common when it comes to those in power like religious pride and desire of wealth."

RELATIVITY AND THE PROBLEM WITH ORGANIZATIONS

In science many doors have opened in regard to understanding relativity; but in religion it clouds the truth in a situation. The way-and-why, although defined in a specific common concept of time and place, is one of subjective realization. Many traits are common to those in power, such as religious pride and a desire for wealth. While these are only two of the most common problems, they are the two witnessed most often when realized by religious leaders. Corrupt common leaders can reveal themselves in many other ways, depending on the norms of the society.

If an angel of God came to the churches in our society as a poor man, would we accept him as an equal brother, or condemn him in bad faith because of the social differences? In the Christian writings we find this bad faith judgment of other's wealth to be a product of evil thoughts, but today we seem to believe that wealth comes as we please God. The Pharisees also accepted this doctrine of materialism. Even a latent acceptance in this materialism is realized in most Christians.

How are we to deal with this problem? We can find the answer if we are sincere about our insight into what we find within ourselves. If we studied and prayed as we should, the church as a whole would have more insight into solving the problems that infect our organizations. The problem breeds not from our organizations, but whether we accept the false things that make us seem "saintly." The Pharisees accepted views that made them look saintly, but this made them rebellious against Jesus' teachings. Many of these view points were grounded in materialism.

Historically, church reformers have been forced out of the main stream by its leaders, while followers have accepted what the powers-that-be have taught. Clearly then, the fault rests not only with the corrupt leaders, but also with the saints that did not examine the truth of the situation. You should realize that those who accept the view of the powers-that-be are blind to what God desires, and in this way are much like those who lead an openly rebellious life before God. People with true religious insight have a profound relationship with God, but their experience becomes tainted as time passes and as other interpretations are applied. Insights are perverted when the individual having the insight makes it more important than each individual's needs and relationship with God. In Jesus' day this happened with the Sabbath. This fervent attitude about concepts causes division and alienation between believers. The attraction then comes from the dogmatic position and loses its true redeeming qualities.

Even today, each sect condemns another to promote a special type of Christianity. Leaders do this as they wish for preeminence within the religious community in this life. The predicaments stemming from this preeminence is inferred in many of the Christian texts. When talking about Christian topics, these corrupt leaders become shallow, as they do not want to contemplate other's viewpoints. They reject the totality of other individuals who will not accept their position, thereby becoming offensive to Christians that have close moral walks with Jesus. The way-and-why is never answered, as it doesn't fit in with a sect's propaganda. The way-and-why is the etymological source of the knowledge and what it meant at the time given, including what God had in mind when giving the enlightenment or revelation to an individual or generation.

"Those that believe the two are the same are blind to their own disbelief."

When we in our sect cannot answer the way-and-why of the Christian text that contradicts our own position, we begin to follow our philosophical founder's mere opinionated positive positions and thereby realize a relationship with a set of dogmatic beliefs, instead of a relationship with Christ. Those that believe the two are the same are blind to their own disbelief.

The way-and-why is not the consideration of important historical facts that puts new light on Christian dogma, but insight that cannot be understood or created as some formal creed. When leaders reinterpret history for their own personal understanding of Christianity, they only divide believers, while leaving followers confused and judgmental. Godly insight must come from within a person and produce a true walk with God.

No written creed or unwritten tradition can dispense the relationship that mankind has searched for throughout history. Sadly, yesterday's insight turns into today's tradition, which turns into tomorrow's creed or unwritten dogmatic beliefs. The original concept may have answered the way-and-why, but creeds and dogmas only point to something beyond the reach of the words written that has been lost by the ever-changing meanings of words. Since the meaning of words gradually change from generation to generation, we constantly need to study to make ourselves approved and to pray and fast in order to know the true will of God. The words in creeds change in meaning over time and the end product is that the dogmatic statements change as well.

INSIGHTS CREATE TRADITIONS

Many Biblical traditions may have come from someone's insight as God reveals the future condition of the Jewish race. But these insights are changed with time as they lose their meaning and emerge as tradition. Instead of the original meaning of the insight, the concept changes into a tradition that can only survive through the interpretation of those in power. Traditions, instead of giving comfort to the Jewish nation (and to us), often inadvertently produce a type of religious bondage that restrains all of us from obtaining the truth of God's will. In so doing it becomes tainted religious dogma that departs from the way-and-why that the insight originally revealed. It merges with some interpretation mixed with Biblical text and becomes a deranged demonic understanding of demeaning dogmatic slavery. This realization can easily be seen in the way the Pharisees acted toward Jesus. They were so bound by their traditions that they could not escape from their own false teachings; as a result they rationalized against the contradictions within their own doctrines when Jesus committed acts that were signs that he was the Messiah, even when those acts were prophesied by their own scriptures. This type of bondage remains alive and active today throughout all organizations. It is written in our creeds and realized in our lives; but it can only endure when we do not overcome it by prayer and studying the meaning of what it is to be Christian.

Authors of the Christian texts used this evolution of simple enlightenments as they declared how religious people had changed the way-and-why knowledge that was given first to the Jews and then to the rest of the human race. One example in the Christian texts puts the disciples and those that followed Jesus in a position of *looking ignorant* and unable to comprehend the parables unless guided by Jesus with his simple explanations of what the stories meant. Even those following Jesus for the wrong reasons were talked about for the purpose of showing some didactic quality. Furthermore, the religious leaders grew angry at Jesus' teachings because they understood what he was implying, even though they didn't accept him as the Messiah. Didactic qualities in Biblical interpretations can bring us to understand the way-and-why of the stories that were written, yet the correct understanding can only come from God revealing the meaning. Knowledge that comes from God is superior to any knowledge that we can learn in church, college, or from reading other books besides the Bible.

There are other teachings of why the different groups of people understood or didn't understand most of what Jesus was teaching. One of these explanations promotes that the disciples had not received the Holy Spirit. This interpretation (easily backed up by the Christian texts) reveals another concept of understanding Christianity if we believe and follow it to its ultimate conclusion. The ultimate conclusion contends that you cannot understand true Christianity or the Bible unless God has given you the insight into the very nature of truth. Although we cannot judge other's hearts, we can grow and become more Christ-like even though so many false teachings that have entered into what is now considered Christianity.

Another interpretation assumes that the Pharisees resisted the Holy Spirit. Yet they must have latently understood Jesus' parables, as it angered them to the point that they wanted him dead, and would murder him if their choices were limited. In this paradoxical confusion, we can only understand when we walk and grow in the Spirit of God. It is beyond knowledge to understand how the Pharisees understood Jesus and at the same time rejected the Holy Spirit.

Furthermore, a third interpretation insists that many were following Jesus so they could get some personal gain, such as the bread and fish or even healings as seen when Jesus healed the ten lepers at one time and only one came back to thank him. The story of the ten healed denotes an antireligious teaching; easily seen if you investigate the story. Or maybe no matter how much you investigate, you will not be able to comprehend the truth unless it is given to you by God.

PAUL THE FIRST THEOLOGIAN

Only Christianity has theologians, as Paul was the first theologian. Every theologian must absolutely believe in the death, burial, and resurrection of Christ. Committing a life that walks in Christ also becomes essential. The problem comes to light when theologians attempt to add more to salvation and sainthood than just the redeeming blood of Jesus. Today theologians discuss the literal truth of the parables, as though existential realization will find increased importance if the stories historically really happened, and be diminished if the parables were only to prove some spiritual concept. Whether the parables happened or not does not make the priority of the lesson change with any degree, unless you want to create a dogmatic belief that only causes division. Paul being the first theologian contended with those that did not have a close walk with God. This contention between the two types of Christians exists even today, but with more worldly generated Christians claiming some fleshly born truth. A worldly generated Christian is one that promotes a dogmatic view as being more important than unity without having enlightenment from God like Paul had on the road to Damascus and throughout his walk afterwards. This division will always be with us as Christianity is existential. This is why Christianity needs theologians and apologists.

The Question must continually find the way-and-why in addition to the information given. You will find a deeper meaning of the Christian text when you commit yourself to understanding the way-and-why. This deeper meaning should transform you, and not make you judgmental against others. They don't understand what you have experienced as no one else could have had the same experiences. The experiences in Christ are individualized and yet should bring us to the same conclusions when we follow the Spirit. This may sound like relativity, but this relativity is founded on a concrete realization of all that exists. Anything that is understood as being relative is grounded in a universal that is based on something that is totally concrete. An example of a universal is that all societies would believe that rape is unethical unless that society was evil. Concrete in this sense would mean, as in the example, that rape is something real.

When the church multiplied with non-Jewish converts, a question arose as to how much Judaism Christianity should inherit. Since Jesus did not condemn Judaism, but in fact supported and obeyed the teachings, this caused the state of affairs concerning Judaism in Christianity to unfold as a difficult question. But after a meeting with Paul and the Apostles, a meeting that did not happen right after Paul's conversion, the question was answered and recorded in the Christian historical text. Since Paul was called to bring the gospel to the other nations, known as Gentiles, he went up to Jerusalem and conferred with the Apostles on the correctness of his teachings. Although we have a clear picture of what the Apostles asked of the Gentiles, some still wished to add more to Christianity, which they believed made every one holier. Even Paul himself didn't condemn Judaism, although he had to fight with those that would make this new sect Jewish. At the same time, Paul would try to teach all that faith in Christ was nothing without the Jews and the Jewish teachings, but this view would cause contention between Christianity and Judaism. The churches belief in the resurrection was a fulfillment of what was probably the main contention between the teachings of the Pharisees and Sadducees. The Church growth infuriated the Pharisees, as Christians claimed the resurrection had already happened, therefore making their Jewish faith void. The resurrection also condemned the Sadducees by suggesting their Jewish belief system was wrong, for Christians claimed to have witnessed the resurrection which the Sadducees denied.

In Christian writings we find that the true church was usually under persecution. However, many would have us believe what we need in order to be accepted by God consists of life's systematic human Biblical interpretations. Both the treatment of the religious leaders and followers, and an understanding of the early churches will produce a clear interpretation that some antireligious phenomenon must have been taking place. This insight doesn't come from some revelation, as many new church organizations would have you believe. These false leaders claim they have received their truth from God through some spiritual religious language. But contrary to false teachings, what a person needs is an enlightenment of the Biblical human condition.

"Whether the stories happened or not does not make the importance of the lesson change in any degree unless you want to create a dogmatic belief that only causes division."

The Biblical human condition we find in the depths of our subjective being: Anguish exists because of our separation from God and anxiety abounds as our finite existence desires to be infinite and therefore we all long for infinity, whether we decide to live in righteousness or commit suicide. Desperation comes into our existence, as the absurdities of life inherently exist in a paradox that makes no sense. We, through communion and fellowship with our God, can find meaning in life. The Bible explains our depravity, which resulted in an existence devoid of a relationship with God, but fortunately the Christian text explains the way to know God, and to experience the phenomenon of salvation. We can find the meaning of life and salvation by what is explained in the Bible through the witness of the prophets of old, but unfortunately many are blind or simply haven't studied,

In every sect we can see someone experiencing a phenomenon of insight, but as individuals begin to learn more about religion or secular philosophy in general, they are forced by the blind to have a relationship with a founder's opinionated positions and leave the true foundation found in a relationship with Christ. Unfortunately, this existential knowledge (that is seen not only in Jewish roots but also in all religious phenomena) becomes interpreted in the wrong light and causes many conflicts instead of what the insight or enlightenment actually meant to produce. Although each of these enlightenments is meant to draw us closer to the truth of godliness, they sometimes lose their purpose. In these cases the enlightenments result in becoming both religious and antireligious. When applied religiously the phenomenon hides its true meaning. In contrast, when it is applied anti-religiously, something is produced that brings an understanding closer to what the world needs both secularly and religiously. One example can be understood by studying the history of the Pharisees. At first they were a group that wanted to help the poor and live by Biblical teachings, but by the time of Jesus' contemporaries, they evolved into self-centered religious leaders that cared more about their religious system and personal power than the people their founders wanted to help. Is this not a reflection of many saints today? Another example maybe found in some Christian organizations that teach that their dogmatic view is more important than those people that have not accepted the organization's doctrine. At first their beliefs were meant to bring individuals closer to Biblical truth, but now those beliefs only make a follower feel more important in an internalized Gnostic way.

If the final teaching produces in you a closer Biblical interpretive light, then a true meaning of the insight has been realized. Jesus' parables do exactly this when correctly interpreted. Not a new light as in a dogmatic teaching, but an understanding of an ethical situation. But this insight can cause pride. When leaving your moral situation behind, you start thinking just like the Pharisees. There exist some types of contentions between those that become Christ-like and those that evolve into Pharisee-like Christians. We therefore find that knowledge brings both types of Bible believers into existence. Unfortunately, the pride comes into play when faith and intellectual knowledge are mixed into a type of faith that is self-centered. So when leaping from faith to faith because of insight we must always realize we are no better than the Gnostic believers. True faith can grow in humility and not pride.

CHRISTIANS AND PHARISEES ARE ALIKE

A dynamic situation led up to the story of the parable of *The Man that Built a Vineyard* that seemed to escalate into a bitter confrontation with the Pharisees. Contributing to the contention was not only just the Pharisees attitude, but also what their religious views represented. The fact that they were Bible believers intensifies the importance for us to understand why Biblical religious followers rejected Jesus' teachings, and what implications this phenomenon has for today's believers. Jewish religious believers understood their worldview from the history and prophesies found in the Bible. Why they went so wrong in Jesus' time and prophetically followed the parable seemingly in accordance with the words of Jesus is important to our understanding, so that we Christians do not commit the same mistake. They also believed they were the true followers of God. What if we are following the same example, not knowing our true nature? And how could we not imitate the Pharisees? Do we emulate them? There are too many parallels between the attitude of Christian leaders and Pharisee leaders to ignore. Remember, Bible believers pushed to have Jesus put to death.

The Bible was definitely an icon and the center of Jewish life. Pharisees not only lived by the Bible with existential meaning, but the Bible also contained their ancestral history. Just like the Jews, most if-not-all Christian organizations use history to teach their foundation for existence. It would seem that the Jews knew the Bible better than almost any Western religious person today. Christianity esteems those who have a well-rounded knowledge of the Bible. Jewish history inherently became more a part of them and their families than it has any Western religious person today who is not a descendent of the Jews. Through faith, Christianity claims to have a spiritual history with Abraham. Even the original majority of the writers and readers of the Christian text were probably descendents of Abraham. Both Jewish and Christian leaders write books and letters on how to live and on their interpretations of the Bible in order to make it easier for all to follow and understand.

Although there are many similarities between modern religious leaders and Jesus' contemporary religious-minded people, we must realize that knowledge has been lost through time. It may be that much of the lost knowledge pertaining to what the Pharisees believed and how they lived will never be recovered and that false assumptions about them will remain forever accepted. Despite this, we can still see that even then their understanding completely tainted their beliefs. Our understanding could just as easily have fallen into error, especially considering that even the first-century churches did not completely keep what constituted the right way to think within the religious condition, with the exception of the persecuted church of Smyrna. The Pharisee's teachings were not altogether wrong, as many Pharisees converted to the ranks of Christianity. Today most Christian teachings reflect Biblical interpretations just as the Pharisee's teachings did in their day.

When Christians are persecuted, they do not argue about creed, tradition and high-minded theological ideas. With freedom of speech, we do this consistently and the results are dividing and weakening our evangelistic efforts. We can easily sit back and condemn the religious believers who rejected Jesus; but didn't Jesus' contemporaries condemn the prophet's killers? No wonder Paul Tillich wrote that *there is a problem when Christian and secular norms are the same*[1]. It is hard to tell the true from false saints when norms are indistinguishable. High minded theological ideas should not be examined by their results, and only accepted as mere logic and systematic thought.

CHRISTIANITY AND THE SECULAR MUST BE DIFFERENT

What happens as we make religious and secular norms one in the same? Acceptance of this norm can grow easily and existentially; it can be found evenly or unevenly between true and false ethical beliefs. During a confrontation, Jesus related to the Pharisees their misunderstanding of what God had intended. Yet, even though the Pharisees knew that Jesus' teachings condemned them, their non-belief in him, or their belief in something else caused them to not accept the truth of the story or stories Jesus told that day. In fact, they set out to do just what Jesus foretold in the parable. But the religious leaders did not feel condemned by the story, because their belief system could not allow them to accept Jesus' authority. Their teachings were so grounded in their cultural and philosophical existence that they internalize its concepts much more than anything Jesus could teach them.

Even after listening and understanding the story, the Pharisees, like Moses' Pharaoh, hardened their hearts and fulfilled what Jesus proclaimed. They did not feel guilty, because their religious teachings clouded their judgment. They set out to kill Jesus, just as the tenants in the story did to the son of the vineyard owner. We can easily see the wrongs of the Pharisees, but we do not easily accept that today's Christians have replaced the Jewish religious leaders as the keepers of God's word. The Temple today consists of one's body. Christian leaders now control the meaning of the word of God. In other words, we now understand Christianity in light of the Biblical interpretations as controlled by those Christians that claim to be leaders. Yet many live as materially rich individuals instead of reflecting the image of the Apostles. This may sound redundant from the above text, but it reveals problems that we in church organizations need to consider through internal means as possible errors in our relationship to our existential walk with God. We should seek an existential walk with God and live our lives before God in both our subjective thoughts in communication with God, and in the physical world around us as we live our daily lives. When we see both of these as a complete whole in relationship to our walk with God, we will live an existential life with God.

Furthermore, some interpretations of Jesus' parables teach that the story has something to do with the Gentles, but with parables that are easily understood and parables that Jesus explains to the disciples, there is never an interpretation that gives incitement to the role of the Gentiles that are in contention with Israel. Neither should we find any interpretations that produce an understanding that can lead to a metaphysical or physical worldview of reality that reflects beyond what we can see for such as a doctrine of heaven and hell. These outlandish explanations are often taught with so much zeal that the true meaning of the story disappears, because it doesn't fit the dynamics of the religious life or organizational dogma. Much of the Bible has typologies, symbolisms and other ways of helping us to have a closer relationship with the Creator, and thereby hiding the lessons' real meaning from those that are not true Christians. Most religious teachers do not want to teach or see an antireligious base for any interpretation and only see a conflict with those that reject their teachings. This not only puts a teacher in an ethnocentric mood, but also becomes blinding to the true teachings of the Biblical text.

PARALLELS BETWEEN CHRISTIANS AND PHARISEES

"Most religious teachers do not want to teach or see an antireligious base for any interpretation and only see a conflict with those that reject their teachings."

Many of the parallels reflected the Pharisee's actions during Jesus' time and without a doubt reflect the same things Christians do today; therefore, parables should be investigated more than what typically we have while researching and studying the Bible. The Pharisees kept the foundations of Judaism as Christians keep the foundation of Christianity. The Pharisees proclaimed they kept the laws of Moses. Christians believe by faith in a salvation that keeps a greater law. It is easy to note that many of those that killed the prophets believed in temple worship. Some were even considered as faithful followers that would not bring into Israel strange Gods, or practices that were not Biblical. They knew themselves as the orthodox Biblical believers. The scriptures stood sacred before them and they lived by its traditions, as they believed they understood the Bible. It is astonishing how much this seems to mirror modern Christianity. We are like the Jews whom unknowingly brought into the temple things that found no acceptance by God and blinded these Bible leaders to the truth.

Can we find parallels between Christian understanding and the way Pharisees thought in reference to the religious life? This parable can bring up personal and serious questions. Is it just as easy to apply this parable to a modern day Christian if we accept Christians as the modern Pharisees? The Religious leaders of that day caused Jesus' well-known crucifixion. They followed the Bible, studied and believed it as the words from God, and built their dogma around it, even down to what constituted correct clothing. They had it written on paper, and lived it daily. They wrote books on the interpretations, and discussed issues of beliefs in the synagogues. So what is the difference between the churches and the synagogues?

Also, did not the Pharisees have a love for the indepth studying of the Bible? The Synagogues reflect the modern day Christian churches. Much of what Christians believe came from Paul, a Pharisee before and even after his conversion. Paul had an indepth understanding not just because he seemed to have a close walk with God, but also his knowledge of Biblical religion that had been realized by him in his past as a Pharisee. Even Paul seemed to condemn the religious people of his time just as Jesus did in the parables. Paul not only rejected the religious living of his past, but also those that would attempt to make Christianity a religion. Those that were religious and Bible believing Jews set out to denounce Paul, just as Paul, before his conversion, attempted to get rid of the saints of his time. Many people do not understand that not only the non-believing Jews were trying to discredit Paul, but also many that believed and wanted to add more to salvation then just Jesus and Him crucified.

To the modern Christian it seems absurd that biblical scholars would set out to harm someone because of their religious beliefs. How could someone who believed in the Christian text set out to stifle someone that didn't agree? That would be like a Baptist trying to execute a Methodist. Except, condemning one another continues to grow in our churches today. The Religious leaders of Jesus' time did that to Jesus and Paul. After all, how did they justify such action? Christian organizations dehumanize others by making their dogma more important than the individual. This dehumanizing of individuals comes from the same spirit that the Pharisees taught.

THE PHARISEES UNBELIEF

The truth probably latently infers that the Pharisees didn't really believe their own religious dogma. Jesus healed people saying their sins were forgiven. The Pharisees taught that an individual was sick or handicapped because of personal sin or sin from someone in the family. These statements, of forgiving sin after healing, did not mean while Jesus healed their bodies he also forgave them of all their sins; but was a direct reference to the dogmatic teachings of the Pharisees concerning sin, that people had physical problems because of sin in the family. By saying this, Jesus used the Pharisees' tradition and dogma against them. The Pharisees own philosophy would claim Jesus as the Messiah and also God for only God can forgive sins. So the Pharisees had to accept that Jesus could forgive sin, as he healed all types of disease. Yet, even by using their own understanding of the Bible, Jesus could not get the Pharisees to see the truth of who he was nor that their doctrine was in error.

Many Christians today rely on their dogma to save them instead of having a relationship with Christ. They, like the Pharisees, put their belief system before the human condition. Doctrine exists for the human race, not the human race for dogma. With all the dogma that exists in the law, it still could not save someone from sin, just as the acceptance of any Christian doctrine cannot save one person. God demanded the same thing from the Pharisees as he does from the Christians and that is found in the dogma written in one's heart.

The Pharisees believed that they knew the will of God. But their faith must have found shallow ground as they refused to transcend into a deeper understanding that was written right before them in their history. They completely rejected the way-and-why. They also had complete systematic belief with no faith. For even the Pharisees needed to repent as much as the sinners and publicans of those days. Instead of going beyond their beliefs, they did not see through the meaning of their teachings and therefore could not find a deeper meaning into their lives. They were so accepting of their understanding of Biblical text and the systematic philosophy of their traditional dogma that they believed that only a leader that believed in their doctrines could be the true Messiah. This true Messiah would bring them political freedom even as they kept others in bondage, for their hearts were self-centered just like those that controlled the vineyard.

Furthermore, the Pharisees were considered as the educated elite and therefore they could not believe that the common person knew much about the spiritual things of the saints, as the common sinner couldn't live accordingly. The Pharisees had faith in their goodness and therefore they didn't have to rely on those that seemed beneath them. Christians today separate themselves according to creed and color of skin. They preach a doctrine of love, but want to stay in small churches of their own kind. The Pharisees found this comfort zone long before Jesus died on the cross. Many Christian leaders today have not searched beyond the understanding of their beliefs to transcend into a relationship of faith in Christ. Jesus inferred that if we truly believed we could make not only a tree die but also a mountain move. The problem with trying to make this saying symbolic comes when we see that Jesus made the tree die in front of the disciples. Christianity has become a religion of beliefs with very shallow faith. Of course, Christian writers talked about miracles even into the third century and even today many Christians talk about healings. Though nothing seemed as simple as Jesus cursing a tree and watching it die, the act causes simple philosophy and theology to become complex. This may not suggest that outward miracles prove salvation, but maybe it shows that a systematic belief system cannot find perfection and that Christianity goes beyond an expression in logical writings or words, but exists in some deep experience that produces faith.

Christians, as people, have a belief structure in order to produce a workable knowledge of Christianity; furthermore, a Christian must have faith that transcends any quality of belief. You can comprehend faith separate from belief. You can have belief without faith, but you cannot have faith without belief. Faith consists of that existential quality which goes beyond belief. Existential faith must come into being and be realized only through experiencing the holiness of Christ. Faith then becomes an inherent part of your being. Your idea of reality is internally shaped by your faith and not something *you will* but something that remains you. In conclusion, faith is something you are, not something you rationalize with your mind.

The Pharisees had a belief structure that caused them to act in a certain way towards Jesus. This seemed mostly negative. They could only believe what they internalized and taught as they could not go beyond their human teachings. In fact, Nicodemus had to come at night to talk to Jesus probably because he didn't want to upset his fellow believers. His coming at night reveals that while in the status quo he did not posses freedom that allowed him to look for something more than what the synagogues (or in our churches today) had to offer. Has the modern church put Christians in a place where they cannot find a deeper understanding of faith? We can only find Biblical answers in life when we search deeper than intellectualism. If intellectualism could save you, then God could have stopped with the Pharisees. Only by experiencing that which the world cannot experience can you find God. Christian faith consists not in dogmatic beliefs or in traditions, as they point to something beyond the words written on paper or thought in the mind. The dogmatic and traditional beliefs in Christianity point to a faith that remains existential in understanding

CHAPTER 2
GOOD SAMARITAN

It is in vain for any man to usurp the name of Christian, without Holiness of life, purity of manners, benignity and meekness of spirit.

John Locke (A Letter Concerning Toleration)

And a highway will be there; it will be called the Way of Holiness. The unclean will not journey on it; it will be for those who walk in that Way; wicked fools will not go about on it.

Isaiah 35: 7-9 (The Bible—New International Version)

WE PARTICIPATE
IN WHAT WE DO NOT BELIEVE

Did you know you have more in common with those that you fight against than those that agree with you? We all seem to have opinions shaped by those that oppose our concepts. Religious concepts that become accepted as correct beliefs often originate from human contention. They then are finally considered equal with the Christian writings, as creeds become the correct interpretation of what the early church thought and believed. When you accept a creed, you quit examining the issue and consider other ideas that shape your beliefs. Many of these creeds can change over time as words seem to change in meaning with every generation. This evolution of changing language has caused many to promote dogma that isn't in line with the correct interpretation of what the Christian writers were trying to teach the church.

The lawyer that questioned Jesus had more in common with the woman at the well than just their disagreement on religious views. For us to understand our own situation we can use both of these people as an example. Many times when someone rebels against another, the person who rebels internalizes a belief that dynamically opposes the other person. These two had an understanding about life that involved each other. They both had strong opinions that came from a traditional ancestral history. We would call that history Biblical. In their existences, they understood the world in reference to what the other one believed. One of the contentions consisted in choosing the proper place to worship; this disagreement between the two religious views grew into a hostile hatred of each other. With this in mind you can see their ways of life indirectly affected each other. The Jews did not mingle with the other nations, and consequently, because of their close Biblical teachings they had a deep hatred for the Samaritans. Because of these Biblical ties the Jewish people established doctrines against the Samaritans that condescended in comparison to other nations.

CHURCHES ARE BUILT ON REBELLION TO OTHER ORGANIZATIONS

Even though the lawyer would not have had anything to do with the woman, both of them believed they participated in doing the right things to please God. Their ancestors both constructed a religious foundation from the same source. Today we see the same manifestation in the human condition as sects come into existence because of contentions about something someone believed. Organized churches split into different sects because of some contention with a belief system. These problems create legalistic views of the subject on both sides of the issue. The fighting divides and confuses those in religious societies, yet, at the same time confirming their dogmatic views. In every belief system the paradox of confusion and confirming evidently exists.

"You have more in common with those that you fight against than those that agree with you."

Many of the sects create a foundation with a systematic theology in reference to what others don't believe. This contention causes the issue to become important. Someone at sometime brought up the disagreement about the difference that started an un-Biblical discussion on the subject. To fight against or condemn a belief system only justifies those that do believe that doctrine and receive such condemnation as a true confirmation of validity. In this we see that contention makes a situation important. Our contentions, created by self-pride, divide us instead of having us working together in Biblical love, and hinder us individually and evangelically.

Most of the Christian texts speak to the individual as the subjective-self and not about how to create lasting dogmatic beliefs. In all the Christian text there may be only one statement of written doctrine that tells Gentiles what they should abstain from in place of following Jewish customs. Should we judge ourselves within or by our creeds that have been handed down by those with many contentions? The reason that the Bible finds relevance today stems from the fact it still speaks to us as individuals and not as a group. God speaks to the believer's subjective-self while the unbeliever is condemned by the objective truth of being.

Bible believers have many religious rites in order to feel accepted by God. Paul wrote about these ways of worship as having a form of righteousness, yet with little benefit in God's kingdom. The Apostle Paul also spoke about not judging others on how they worship, but we establish different sects within Christianity exactly for this reason. Don't we all have views that make sense to us and forget that others have different views that make sense to them, even though we use the same book? This contradiction, formed from our self-centeredness or some contrary spirit, should not exist among us that read from a book that teaches us to love one another. Paul stated that we should all grow together, but we can't as long as we center our thoughts on the differences and contentions between our viewpoints, which only cause *wars, and rumors of wars among us.*

Jesus seemed to condemn both Jewish and Samaritan's belief systems as he searched for something profound in each individual. This profound subject of belief that Jesus looked for consisted in existential holiness, and therefore has critical importance in understanding the Bible, for many still believe in a false type of holiness. A true type of holiness as seen in the story of the woman caught in adultery finds its place not in outward dress, but subject thought as Jesus spoke to the crowd. Jesus first talked to the crowd making them look at their own lack of holiness and then, lastly, he talked to the woman in order for her to also see the lack of her holiness. We ourselves need to examine our belief systems and not use our knowledge against others. But isn't it easier for us to condemn others instead of looking at our own depravity? Many people do not realize that they judge others differently than they judge their friends and themselves. By doing this we naturally exist as workers of iniquity. When understanding this train of thought existentially, we internalize the teachings of the aforementioned story and learn the true definition of holiness.

HOLINESS: NOT A DRESS CODE

There are many different ideas on what constitutes holiness. What are the different views of holiness? Where does true holiness come from? Jesus was teaching others to find it within their subjective-selves. Holiness comes from God and produces righteousness. We through religion seem to create holiness within that produces righteousness, but the truth is that the opposite happens. Experiencing God as holy within us changes us. Both the lawyer and the Samaritan woman became subjects of this concept and learned it subjectively by coming into contact with Jesus. Holiness is subjective and therefore existential. Objective holiness can only be a shadow or symbol of holiness, or something all together different. All outward holiness exists as self-righteousness and develops demonically. When we understand this, we can become open to experiences that change our lives. The most important example would be John the Baptist, probably the holiest of all men.

"If we do not doubt and examine ourselves than we really don't believe."

TRADITIONAL PARABLE NAMING IS A MISTAKE

Traditionally a story is given a name, but that name can often hide the true meaning, even though the title may be descriptive. Unfortunately, all parables are given a title that is considered descriptive. Like the *Prodigal Son* that takes the focus off of other characters, the *Good Samaritan* hides some of its true meaning by putting the focus on the Samaritan's good will and hiding the audience's reactions to all the other characters. Traditional naming which changes the meaning of the parables occurs in many of the teachings of Jesus. If the parables were not titled, we might have a deeper understanding of the Gospels. It becomes less than pragmatic when we accept in blind faith what interpretation is offered merely because present authority believes in that understanding. We are taught it is nobler to examine teachings, but at the same time this is discouraged in practice. The confusion comes when we question the tradition that the leaders believe, for this translates into questioning the leadership. True criticism seeks to find the real meaning behind the Biblical stories which may bring about the discarding of tradition, authority, and modern trains of thought.

Science gave us the insight to doubt all things, a methodology that exists latently in the Christian writings. We cannot have faith without doubt for we consist of spirit and flesh. If we do not doubt and examine ourselves then we really don't believe but have just accepted views advanced by authoritative teachers. When did you last examine your thinking rather than examining your actions in light of the Bible? The human condition forces us to judge by outward appearances, as we cannot see others' subjective-selves. We also groom ourselves outwardly to look acceptable with what we think emulates holiness. Our actions speak louder than our words as we groom ourselves in order to be judged appropriately. This outward concern creates contention between our flesh and spirit if we examine ourselves in reference to the Bible.

Science now follows this Christian example of not doubting with reference to the Theory of Evolution, where politically correct mainstream science has quit doubting and now accepts a theory as fact even though other explanations exist. When science commits this sort of act they turn scientific speculation into religious dogma. Of course, unlike some Christians whom will give up their outdated creeds, these scientists will never accept their contradiction for they will not give up their atheistic worldview. Another fallacy in science exists that teaches putting God in an equation doesn't change the results. Although this is true in some theories, we can see that science cannot rule out a God, so it must take God into account with some hypothesis. By denying an equation with a creator, science has forfeited the view to doubt all things. Atheism must also be doubted. Atheism must be viewed as a philosophical position and should find a strong rejection among the scientific community that desires to investigate unbiased nonpolitical facts that only true scientific speculation strives to achieve.

WHEN DOUBTING IS GOOD

Did the widow with her mites give more because of her greater percentage? She gave out of her needs while others gave from their excessive wealth. They gave from their heart, but she gave what she needed for that day. The current secular teaching is that what comes from one's heart may be important; this truth should be studied in more detail than just the acceptance of the phrase. Any statement should be examined over and over again just as any interpretation should be studied from a negative approach, not a positive reinforcement. You may be sincere with your positive reinforcement, but that will never make the belief system correct. We can hide behind a spirit like those that gave much that day or we can examine the situation as the disciples learned to do through Jesus' teachings.

The Pharisees did good deeds throughout the community, believing they helped others through a good heart. Many of the teachings of the Bible become misdirected as holy secular thought develops into holy Biblical speculation and interpretation. Jesus confronted the Pharisees concerning this issue just as we should examine our many secular views of today. We think they are Biblical just as the Pharisees believed their philosophical system was Biblically sound. Belief systems that come from the Bible inherit Biblical grounding, but we should not blindly accept these views even though they find their roots in Bible contemplation. Understandings may be based on the Bible, but not existentially correct. Just as we can add lemons to water to make lemonade, we can also add Biblical words and phrases to a belief system and it becomes Biblical, but that doesn't mean the teachings add up to correct Biblical concepts.

Jesus did not say the poor widow gave from her heart or that she gave a higher percentage than the others, but taught the disciples that she gave from her future needs and the others gave from their abundant past. Jesus spoke to the religious leaders of his time and told them *they worshiped God in vain because they taught doctrines of men calling these beliefs God's doctrines.*

Their teachings consisted of an outward holiness with no inward roots. Do the religious teachers of today follow this same path without knowing that they emulate those religious teachers that crucified Jesus? A misconception comes from believing the Jews crucified Jesus. But without a doubt a correct understanding would see that the Bible teaches that those who controlled the religious beliefs in that day were the ones that crucified Jesus, and those that did not follow their ways found themselves as outcast. This observation examined correctly in the light of what Christianity is and also how to act as a Christian will find an important part in deep-rooted holiness.

A LESSON FROM THE WELL

Jesus spoke directly to another woman much like the outcast poor woman. The widow who gave her mites at the temple found herself an outcast because of her poverty. The Jewish ethnic prejudice against the Samaritan made an outcast of the woman at the well. That she also had issues within her own culture is evident in her coming to the well alone instead of when all the other women came to socialize. It would seem that in the Christian view no outcasts should exist, but we all push away others and make up excuses as to why these outcasts don't belong. We state this rejection has nothing to do with our Christian perspective of life, or we claim we must reject those that we push away since our religious views will not let us accept society's rejects; by justifying this behavior we bring a dog pack worldview into our Christianity. The Pharisees surely taught that the poor received little of any blessing from God and were only a little more human than a Samaritan. But these outcasts were mysteriously drawn to Jesus. They anticipated his Messiah-ship.

This displeased the Pharisees as they thought the Messiah should accept what they accepted and reject what they rejected. They were also displeased that the common person believed Jesus was the Messiah, or at least a prophet from God. We exhibit this same attitude today. We, like the Pharisees, accept the successful person as blessed by God and think of those going through rough times as under God's judgment that will make them better Christians. Or perhaps such people cannot take care of little things, so God does not promote them with better worldly possessions. This attitude prevails within the ranks of Christianity even though none of the Apostles died rich.

The Samaritan woman represented a religion that was contrary to and hated by the Jews. They despised the Samaritans more than the Gentiles. The Samaritans had a rich religious background that both historically fought against and at other times with the Jewish nation. They used some of the Bible and their own history to establish their religious beliefs. Many places where the Samaritans lived remained holy to the Jewish nation because of their historically Biblical references. Information about the Samaritans unfortunately seems lost to history.

But modern controversies about Samaritan's beliefs do not diminish any of the truths Jesus revealed by using the Jews' dislike of the Samaritans to teach the disciples the right way to think. Jesus taught his disciples the holiness of the Samaritan's religion through the woman, and illustrated to the Pharisees their holiness by using a Samaritan as a good example. Jesus uses people's own prejudices as a tool, as these prejudices come from an incorrect understanding of Biblical holiness. In contrast, the different sects of the Jewish nation used prejudices to establish their superiority over other belief systems and people. The human condition reveals its evil self with this attitude today as we see many people dying through what is called ethnic cleansing. Grave danger grows when we accept our holiness status as being more important than individuals. When do we not help someone because helping seemed against our religious beliefs or we even withdrew from someone whose belief system dynamically opposed our faith? This question should be answered subjectively.

HOLINESS REVEALED

Holiness exists in the inward person. The woman showed her holiness when she did not lie to Jesus about her present condition. The condition of holiness within the woman bridged the gap between her religious and righteous life. We must understand that even though she was an outcast because of her life, her holiness was no better or worse than those today accepted in society and religious circles as being Godly. Even though some knowledge has been lost concerning the Samaritans, we can still infer that they had a rich religious tradition. We today accept others first by the way they look and second by their wealth. We therefore find ourselves guilty of judging outwardly and forgetting that we cannot see the inward person.

Holiness is existential and not some knowledge or physical object. In the same respect the lawyer proclaimed his holiness as he honestly answered Jesus' question. The lawyer probably believed that holiness resides in dress, manners, and religious rites, as well as in other artifacts referenced in the Jewish teachings. But Jesus let the lawyer illustrate his own holiness indirectly through searching for the answer to the question concerning his neighbor. When reading the Christian writings, many forget that some Pharisees did accept the faith and most of the Christian texts came from an educated Pharisee. We assume the lawyer may be a Pharisee. But we can easily take him as a type of someone that confesses to know the Bible.

EVEN WRONG BELIEFS ARE BIBLICAL IF THEY COME FROM THE BIBLE

Jews despised the Samaritans because their religious views sprang from a Biblical basis. The Samaritans probably taught that their Biblical interpretation was correct even though completely contrary to the Jewish teachings; the Samaritan woman at the well knew of this contention between the Samaritans and the Jews. Many questions asked of Jesus for the wrong reasons set the spirit of the questioning from Jesus in motion. This argument between Jews and Samaritans most likely came from a long history of dislike for each another. The Samaritans with their Biblical landmarks could have known some concept of the holy. They probably accepted these landmarks as holy places because holy men built or did something there, and therefore the Samaritans could have built their religion around these places. Logically, if one religion taught the truth correctly then the other must be wrong. The Samaritan woman most likely tried to find out from Jesus, since he was a Jew, his position on the argument as if he might agree with her beliefs, as his associated with her. Maybe she thought Jesus might also live as an outcast since he spoke to her, for the communications between the Jews and Samaritans had many complications.

"Dogmatic views cannot make you righteous."

It was especially strange to find Jesus meeting this woman at this time of day; no wonder questions were asked. Yet, Jesus looked for holiness in people. Both the Jew and the Samaritan, as well as other religions, tend to seek what can be found as holy and worthy of God's pleasures. If this were not true in relationship to her religious life, then the woman would never have desired to ask the question. Dogma becomes the outcome of such searching, but holiness bridges the gap between righteousness and religiousness in experiences. Righteousness can never separate itself from religion, but many religions exist with no righteousness. Dogmatic views cannot make you righteous. The only thing that makes you righteous comes from subjective holiness through the blood of Christ. The woman was looking for some intellectual understanding and Jesus gave her an ethical viewpoint. Intellectual views create division as holiness creates unity.

COMMONALITY OF RELIGION, RIGHTEOUSNESS AND HOLINESS

Something exists within religion that creates righteousness and this concept manifests itself as the practice we call holiness. We may conclude that most dogmas, written or oral, point to something good, but teachers need to create an atmosphere in which we transcend faith in dogma until we produce holiness. Therefore dogma takes place as symbolic language and points to truth. For dogma can only become stagnated and adulterous when transformed into the object of worship in place of God, as all doctrine loses its symbolic language. We confuse this issue by believing that the acknowledgement of dogmatic beliefs pleases God. Putting dogma before charity creates that which grows into something unholy. This is what blossomed into the mistake of the religious Jewish teachers and also is our mistake as Christians today. Regardless of whether we admit it or not, our dogmatic views have become a part of our being.

Jesus said to the Samaritan woman at the well, *"we know whom we worship and you do not know because salvation is of the Jews."* This does not affirm that the religious Jewish teachers of Jesus' time had their beliefs correct, but is an indication of what was a problematic concept for the Samaritan's teachers. The Samaritan's religious grounds for existence, without their Jewish counterparts, probably remained shallow, as also Christianity cannot subsist without the Jewish foundation. The Samaritans surely found no way to explain the coming of the Messiah being a child of David. They couldn't understand what God planned for humanity, as their symbolism contained no life in their practices. More than likely the Samaritans didn't acquire much of a foundation with regard to the Bible and probably only kept landmarks with some history. Many of us, like Samaritans, accept what the leaders in our organization teach while rejecting what others believe without learning and judging everything we can on the issues. We do this as our flesh wishes to find favor with those that seem like Christian leaders within an organization.

Jesus' statement could not have been one of conformation because of His story of *The Good Samaritan* that condemned the Pharisee's basic view that they remained the children of God because they came from Abraham's seed. This story cuts to the core problem with the religious teachings of Jesus' time. The questions concerning what it mean to be a child of Abraham remains a key issue within the context of religion. All Jews born through Abraham remain his children but not because of religious identity. No religious Jewish organization should claim to be more Jewish than any other Israelite. But Christianity contends that Abraham's seed also occurs by faith even though no natural bloodline exists.

The answer to who can claim Abraham as father finds realization in knowing true inward holiness. For true holiness lives not in intellectual concepts, but enlightenment from experience, for you can only realize holiness. You can neither see nor touch holiness. When Jesus attacked the accepted Biblical teachings of his day, he looked for inward holiness and not to prove that his understanding prevailed, as the prevailing religious teachings lost any true knowledge of God. When Moses took off his shoes because of holy ground, the ground was holy only because the presence of God was there. When God had stopped manifesting himself in that place, the ground was no holier than someone's backyard. You must have the Spirit of truth inside you to be holy.

THE MOST ANTIRELIGIOUS PARABLE

This struggle between the two belief systems makes the Good Samaritan the most antireligious of all the parables.

The Samaritan, who was the good guy, would have been hard for the Pharisees to accept. A Samaritan could not have any part of the inheritance of God. This can be seen by Jesus' statement of salvation coming from the Jews. This was a direct attack also against the Samaritan's religious history. The Samaritans would have had a hard time explaining that their beliefs were right without acknowledging the need of the Jewish bloodline. Or else their beliefs must have by-passed any kind of understanding of a Messiah. We may never know unless more evidence is found to support what the Samaritans believed, even though some evidence has been discovered. And this evidence would not change the meaning of what it is to be Christian.

In this story, Jesus also condemns the religious beliefs of the Jews as they would not defile themselves to help someone in need. Any dogma that is more important than human needs is anti-holy at best and without a doubt demonic. The Pharisees knew this, but refused to deny their faith in their written and oral beliefs. We also define our beliefs in the same appeal to systematic concepts as the Pharisees did with their faith. This causes our concept of the holy to be distorted. Their concept of the holy could only be seen in the observances of dress, objects, and written and oral traditions. We do the same today; many Christians even go to the holy land hoping to find some concept of the holy. Or we dress, act and talk a certain way with the belief that we are somehow holier.

When Jesus told the lawyer the parable, it would have been a little confusing for him, as the lawyer would have had a dislike for what was taught because of his racist views. It would have rubbed against his conscience when he acknowledged the Samaritan as the righteous one. The lawyer could have stuck to his racist beliefs about the Samaritans and refused to answer the question; he could have complained about the meaning and justification of following the law and the importance of not being defiled. He also could have believed that the individual that needed attention fell into God's punishment, which is not only something that may have been believed by the Pharisees, but by some Christians today. Even though Jesus healed the sick and raised the dead, which dogmatically meant to the Pharisees that sins were being forgiven, the Pharisees still could not accept him as the Messiah for it would contradict other teachings that were handed down from tradition. As we read the account, it may seem absurd for us today. But how many of our traditions are handed down that may or do blind us from the truth? We may never know until it is too late. Unfortunately, as in Jesus' time, we are discouraged from investigating. Is this so because we have become just like the Pharisees? Are we not as stiff-necked as those before us?

The lawyer, who was probably looking to trick Jesus into accepting his racist viewpoint, revealed his honesty with his answer. The lawyer probably would have been even more opposed to the acceptance that Jesus gave the Samaritan woman, yet this lawyer's answer was a sign of his holiness, and was the bridge between his righteous and religious life. It was not the ritualistic holiness of an object or action as taught by those that understand an outward type of religion, but that transcending quality that bridges the gap between righteousness and religion. As a lawyer, his job was to understand the Biblical concepts like holiness; but he didn't understand that those that were in the Spirit, and not some higher human wisdom, wrote the Bible. We today tend to gravitate towards those that seem to be great speakers and towards leaders with knowledge that amazes us while giving us the sense that we are becoming more spiritual by learning from them.

HOLINESS IS WITHIN

Problems arise as we realize there are many religious interpretations with respect to the Bible. The lawyer probably had firsthand knowledge that has been lost concerning the multiple problems between the Jews and the Samaritans. But this knowledge is not important as Samaritans eventually found salvation through the Jews. In fact, they came into Christianity before the Gentiles, revealing the power of God when we consider that the majority of leaders during the beginning of Christianity were Pharisees. This absence of conflict was made possible by something that transcends religious beliefs, which we now categorize as inward holiness. This inward holiness becomes more personally transcendent as we experience the holiness that comes from God; outward religious holiness can never display unity. Inward holiness throws contentions towards non-being, while being grounded in love will produce true unity.

You must look for holiness within each person and avoid that holiness in religious dogma or oral practice as an acceptable form of what is right. Religion can stop you from obtaining salvation if you refuse to learn what holiness is. Holiness is not obtained by keeping false concepts of separating yourself from the world, but by looking objectively for a work of God. In the Bible, objects of holiness proclaimed types and shadows of things to come; but objects can never be holy just as the blood of animals could never forgive sin. Holiness means separation, but this separation is inward and not outward. You do not become more or less holy by going somewhere, or through participating in religious rituals. Those that do this appease their conscience through an emotional thrill while being the center of attraction, which is not holiness but self-centeredness. In this the error is trying to display what should be sought after.

When viewing holiness as outward dressing or places to go and not to go, or even as a way to communicate, these actions turn into a written dogma or an oral tradition and become shallow and stagnated. Then these beliefs through time are worshipped and put on the same standard of holiness with the Bible and considered just as sacred. Even though this belief is orally denied, it is, never the less, practiced in all religions and more so in Christianity. The deceptions of such practices become difficult to detect when they are accepted as social norms within the religious circle. This phenomenon of evolving religious values into concrete social Christian norms exist because it is easier for the human condition to accept outward showings of faith than to follow a subjective relationship with God.

DOGMATIC BELIEFS
DO MORE HARM THAN GOOD

Do you understand Christianity as a set of creeds and doctrinal beliefs that secure a correct way to think, or as a deep personal relationship with the One that died on the Cross and rose to everlasting life? Sects begin to worship dogmatic beliefs and teach that if you don't believe according to what they say is important, you are not really Christian, and you are judged accordingly by those of doctrinal faith. These judgmental dogmas, when accepted as being holy enlightenments from God, are no longer seen as judgmental, but are considered godly truths. This is how false teachers, disguised as Christians, keep you in contact with their historical past. They elevate some concept above others and make you, the follower, believe you are better if you believe them. They may basely look down on those that don't accept their new revelation or enlightenment of their new, but old, religious belief. They confess that they possess an understanding of some truth that has been lost through time, but God has revealed it again so that you, the true church, can be more holy and more dogmatically correct without having to grow in the fruit of the Spirit and realize any inward holiness. Christians should look at history and consider what has been kept alive in holiness with regard to its relationship between religiousness and righteousness. With this understanding of holiness you can experience that which is holy in your simple walk with God while shedding judgmental attitudes that are nothing less than demonic. All doctrine becomes demonic when not stitched together by the fruit of the Spirit. Not demonic as in a fallen spirit, but as in something that is less than Godly love.

Christianity has become a synthesis of the attitudes of the Pharisee, Sadducee and Samaritan's religious viewpoints concerning the Bible. Although Paul was a Pharisee and wrote most of the Christian writings in the light of his understanding of the world through his relationship with God, many of his ways of understanding the Bible would not be accepted in today's fundamental, evangelical or liberal circles. The Pharisees believed not only the written word but also in the interpretation of them and how to apply them to everyday life. The Sadducees believed in the first five books of the Bible and their life was centered on the temple and its meaning to Israel. And the Samaritans had their own understanding of Biblical religion and history.

Pharisees had an oral and written tradition that could make everyday life understood in light of following the laws. The oral and written tradition had just as much authority as the Bible. Concepts were holy to the Pharisees and following the separatist way was a priority that made you holy. Although the Christian faith is built on the interpretations of the Bible, most Christians would say they deny that any other writings are inspired like the Bible. But within Christianity there are always new books being written that have a profound effect on a Biblical aspect of Christianity and there are many books written that tell different sects of Christians how to think and what to believe in everyday life. The Pharisees had their books and we have our books. Most Christians would not accept these other writings as equal in authority to Scriptures or even consider them God-breathed; never-the-less, Christians of all sects treat this group of writings as such and will quote from the authors of profound writings in order to express a religious view. Christians, in fact, elevate these books to the position of authority just as the Pharisees elevated their written and oral traditions.

Is it an error to quote from these books? Maybe not, but one important thing to realize is that what Christianity now teaches it means to be God-inspired and what the Jewish religions of Jesus' time believed that meant are two different concepts. This is important because although Christians preserved most of the letters from Paul and other manuscripts, what these authors thought about their personal writings is probably not the same as how we modern Christians look at those writings today. Why is this important? Because we cannot show through logic or systematic thought what is the truth, but can only find it through God opening up our eyes to true holiness.

BETTER UNDERSTANDING

By understanding other Christian sects you can also understand the errors of your own paradigm of existence. Doesn't Christianity also have its spoken and non-spoken traditions? Yes, if you follow one of these Christian speakers, you become holy and more acceptable to the religious circle and God. That is the Christian's understanding of the sect's beliefs. When you learn the spoken and non-spoken tradition of other Christian sects, it should open your eyes, as this knowledge should enable you to understand that you do the same in your sect that others do in theirs. Human nature makes things fit and thereby make sense of the world and all that we see and know. This fitting together in our mind we call ontological truth. By understanding what some other sect believes, you can become more critical of your own interpretation. If you don't question what you believe then you don't really believe it, but you use the knowledge of your belief system so that you don't have to consider it; the studying of it would take up your time that you desire to use for your pleasures. This learning may lead you into a better understanding of what the Biblical author was trying to teach. Did not Jesus understand the religion of the Pharisees, Sadducees and Samaritans? Through this comprehension Jesus tried to open up the religious individual's mind to existential errors.

Sadducees taught a realistic understanding of what was important concerning the implementation of the commandments. They did not consider the resurrection or study angels. Since Christianity is based on a Pharisee's concept of religion, the Sadducees' role is misunderstood in regard to Israel. But the Sadducees represent the power, authority and foundation of the temple. The Sadducees main concern consisted in the daily rites and holy ways in respect to the objects in the temple. This made the oral and written traditions unacceptable because it added nothing to the Temple worship. Angels, heaven, and hell served them no purpose, as did the belief in a resurrection. Their beliefs were concerned with what the Temple illustrated in the life for the Jews. That was their concept of holy. Holiness was probably only seen imbedded in rituals and objects of the temple in the minds of the Sadducees. There are Christians today who believe going to church and being religious will give them some acceptance by God. They accept the authority of those in power and believe the concepts that are taught are holy. When they think of Christianity, all they can see is the holy building before them and the things of God within that building. Only through the Spirit can you realize your misunderstanding of this faith in holiness. So many who claim to follow Christ are led away by the misdirection inherent in the Sadducees worldview.

Furthering this train of thought, the Samaritans may represent unorthodox types of Christianity. There are those sects that are religious and find some truth in the historical belief of Christianity and claim it to be holy. This is what the Samaritans probably did with their religion. Many Christian sects attempt to illustrate through history and systematic thought that their belief is more sacred and the paradigm that they proclaim is what the Apostles taught. If you can imagine the Sadducees as a type of Christian fundamentalist, and the Pharisees as liberal, then the Samaritan's religion could be those non-orthodox sects that teach their own interpretation of Christianity. We all are looking for that holy truth and believe we have the answer in some aspect through our sect or way of worship. And within any sect you can find all three different aspects of a religious life. Religious minded people have not changed through time. The words used are different but the attitude remains, for we are human. This attitude can also be seen in many religions that are not Biblically based, as we all are looking for the infinite part of our existence.

Furthermore, there are books written that tell us about the symbolic understanding of the rites that are performed in Christianity. The Sadducees were descendents of the Levites, and the Pharisees believed they were the children of Abraham, and that is what saved each individual group. As Christians we also believe we are the spiritual children of Abraham, for we believe by faith. The problem is that this kind of thought changes from faith to dogma in a short time and becomes a phrase that is only echoed but not realized within us. Christians want to rely on dogmatic interpretations of the scriptures. Even the concept of faith is a concern of dogma. Although this must be done in order to understand Paul's writings, Christianity in-depth must be experienced existentially in order to possess the entire claim to be Christian. Neither religious emotions, nor feelings, nor an understanding of dogma, but the experiencing of the holy manifests a closer relationship with God.

EXPERIENCE HOLINESS

You can only experience the Holy when you transcend the religious life and experience the righteousness that is whole, not part of the self before and with God. You experience it when you have fellowship with the Spirit, whose nature is holy. This means that you are not holy unless your righteousness comes from God and not from self-discipline. Self-discipline is not holy, but illustrates a good Christian example. Many religions and even Christianity have examples of self-discipline, but that doesn't make them holy. If you do not understand the difference between subjective and objective holiness, you may never be able to experience the holiness that can only be experienced by existentially knowing Christ.

Furthermore, righteousness is that transcendent quality created by God through our religion. Since Jesus is the only way, righteousness can only come through him, and this righteousness will create holiness. All other righteousness does not create true holiness and therefore is adulterous, for this righteousness is mixed with existential pride. While Peter walked, his shadow healed the sick; he probably was thinking, "Why me and not some other apostle? They didn't deny Jesus three times!" Paul probably thought about how he persecuted the church as he worked wonders. Their attitude implies that holiness is subjective and true holiness is built on Jesus.

We all can easily forsake a subjective relationship with God and replace it with an objective relationship with dogma, as human nature takes the Holy and attempts to change it into dogmatic dress codes and living standards, leaving behind a quality of existential holiness. Holiness is not how you dress and where you go, but it is subjective in what you are becoming through Christ. What qualities you hold on to will define your holiness as you react according to your changing nature. Yet this changing nature can only be found through God. Your nature, that only God can change, is the existential ground of being; therefore, this subjective part of your sinful nature brings you anxiety and loneliness and causes those deep emotional possibilities. True holiness manifests itself when acting in such a way that you treat others as you wish to be treated without realizing or forcing the self to do well. True holiness is revealed in your personality.

The important thing regarding these stories is that they both begin with a discussion on eternal life; the first ends with a definition of a good neighbor and the second ends with a discussion on being satisfied with life. In conclusion, we learn the qualities of being a good neighbor and realize a good life by serving others is founded in understanding eternal life. Being a good neighbor doesn't give you eternal life, but those that have eternal life will become better neighbors. You can become a good neighbor through the Spirit, as you can only have a fulfilled life through being Godly and serving others. In this we can experience holiness.

As with the woman at the well, Jesus was looking for her actions in relationship to what he was asking. The question imposed on her was a religious one, just as the question to the lawyer. The woman accepted him as a prophet, but the lawyer could not accept his teachings even though the lawyer understood Jesus' position. Both woman and lawyer answered Jesus' question with subjective holiness that condemns and acknowledges their beliefs. They both found an answer from a subjective enlightenment and Jesus, by revealing true holiness, let them condemn their religious viewpoints by contradicting their dogmatic position. By answering the questions correctly, they not only condemned their beliefs but also revealed their inward holiness. This way of contradiction by Jesus' questions is a norm and can also be seen in other stories in the Bible. Paul also used types of everyday life to explain the non-tangible things of Christianity, although he did not use parables, as holiness can only be explained abstractly.

"We all easily forsake a subjective relationship with God and replace it with an objective relationship with dogma."

These were two people who each had a Biblically-based sect, but were opposed to one another's beliefs. Even the reaction to each one's acceptance of what was taught by Jesus was different. Their reaction didn't have as much of a bearing on what was wrong with their religious dogma as it was an insight into their righteousness. This righteousness is a transcendent quality of religion. Many people are religious with no righteousness that produces holiness.

The Hebrew's historical holiness was given to objects and people that were set apart for the work of God, representing only types and shadows of what is true holiness. True holiness was and still is that which combines the religious and the righteousness of man. It will always be internal and all encompassing. It is not a part of nor a separate transcendent quality, but that transcendent quality which bridges the gap between righteousness and religiousness. It will always be the transcendent quality that combines these concepts, as righteousness cannot exist by itself without religion, just as holiness cannot exist if religion does not have a transcendent quality that produces righteousness. For holiness cannot be separated from any of these parts; for it is the whole of both righteousness and religion, and is that quality that creates righteousness within religion.

You now should see how the lawyer was linked with the woman at the well and how Jesus may have been really looking for something more profound in their beliefs. This can be seen because of the questions he asked. The questions both condemned their beliefs and taught them what was important. There are different understandings of holiness. But true holiness comes from God and can only be realized through Christ. True holiness can only come from God and this is what produces righteousness.

Religion is not bad by itself, but it is the teachers that make it demonic by denying the need of holiness that is existential. As religion creates holiness within, holiness then produces righteousness. One experiences God and is changed existentially by experiencing the holy. The lawyer and the Samaritan woman had to experience the holy within them as they answered Jesus' questions and chose to accept or reject Him. William James wrote something to the effect that *if everyone experienced a conversion, taught by most Christian sects, the world would be a better place, even if the experience changed them little into following the faith* and this follows as any contact with the holy will change an individual.

CHAPTER 3
THE VIRGINS AND THE TALENTS

For the time will come when men will not put up with sound doctrine. Instead, to suit their own desires, they will gather around them a great number of teachers to say what their itching ears want to hear.

Timothy

And it was a notable observation of a wise father, and no less ingenuously confessed; that those which held and persuaded pressure of consciences, were commonly interested therein, themselves, for their own ends.

Francis Bacon (The Essays)

It is dangerous to be right in matters on which the established authorities are wrong.

Voltaire
("Catalogue pour la plupart des écrivains français qui ont paru dans Le Siècle de Louis XIV, pour servir à l'histoire littéraire de ce temps," Le Siècle de Louis XIV)

WHO WAS JESUS ADDRESSING

Most errors in understanding the parables develop when the reader hasn't taken into consideration the audiences that Jesus addressed. For that reason there are many different interpretations, and while those explanations may establish a good lesson in ethics, they may not reflect the content of Jesus' teachings. So with the content being taken out of place, the context changes according to how we interpret our own experiences as we apply this knowledge to Biblical stories. This is the human condition that helps make sense of the world. Unfortunately, it is easy to misunderstand the story when trying to comprehend it through our own experiences, and how the story applies to the self. Our past learning experiences can blind us to the truth of a parable, especially when we have been instructed incorrectly and base our experiences on false teachings.

Even when we think of the Gospels as the tradition of the early church, what traditions the church tried to preserve can be misleading until we understand the religious issues of those days. Today our thoughts are different from those of Jesus' time. It is hard for anyone to understand what life was like or how people thought in the first century. The way the individual thought and his or her worldview was much different than our views and understanding of the universe today. For instance, today we understand the concept of electricity and many other technologies that make life easier. Even if we live somewhere without these technologies, we still retain knowledge of its applications. We know there are eight known planets, and that the sun is the center of this solar system. We also know that we are only one of the many galaxies in the universe. For many of these reasons, we may never really understand what the early church believed about themselves. If nothing else, our understanding will be tainted.

During Jesus' life, people had to prepare for the seasons. Many of the cultural traditions were based on what could be accomplished during each season. Not only what could be done, but also what had to be done to preserve life. Children also had to work and grow up fast in ancient times. People died at home where they grew up, whereas today we are a death-denying society. Now people die in hospitals or nursing homes and not in familiar surroundings as was the standard practice before the so-called modern age. Although today many teach that back then they had little regard for life, this regard- for-life concept may be very misleading when you consider all they did to preserve the community. The Gospels were an attempt to preserve the community called the *Way,* and what we know today as the church community. Not the buildings or land or religious objects, but those people that participated in the community of saints. The letters in the Christian text can also be looked at as a way of preserving the church traditions, but they were written to teach saints how to live and believe in Jesus.

THE IMPORTANCE OF PAUL

"Paul had a problem of speaking to the Jewish and Gentile converts in explaining how the church functioned."

During the first century of the church, Paul wrote letters to the various churches and individuals instructing them to exemplify Christ. Because Paul believed that faith in Jesus saved and not religious ritual, he attempted to teach them the way to live and think in a perverse generation, just as Peter instructed the crowd to *save themselves* on the day of Pentecost. These teachings of Paul and Peter have been corrupted by modern thought as individuals do not look into all aspects of knowledge. Pentecostalism is one such uninvestigated issue. The first century church would have never have taken the name Pentecostal.

Most people called Pentecostals, who often manifest speaking in other languages and following physical manifestations of the Spirit, do not understand the Jewish celebration. Paul had a problem of speaking to the Jewish and Gentile converts in explaining church functions. He would have understood the parables that referred to the traditions in the Jewish life style, even though today there are many modern day thoughts that teach Paul didn't know the Gospel stories. *The Ten Virgins* are one of those stories with Jewish roots, although Paul never commented on any parable, but quotes Jesus with words not found in the Gospels. Just as Paul used Greek and Roman concepts to explain the church, Jesus used many of the Jewish traditions and teachings in his parables. This fusion of two different social norms seems to have caused issues within the early church, and is one reason it is important to understand Paul.

> **"Since early Christian authorities did not make this distinction, theologians today should consider it suspect."**

Paul wrote most of the Christian texts that were gathered, accepted and preserved by some believers during Paul's life, as he was considered the author. Modern-day theologians contend that there are two kinds of Paul's writings. One type of letter is considered Pauline and the other pseudo-Pauline. The type of information that decides which group a letter functions under and is considered to represent is its eschatological inferences. The Pauline letters suggest that the Lord was coming soon in the first century. Therefore, it is thought that the pseudo-Pauline letters infer that the second coming will be in the distant future. Since early Christian authorities did not make this distinction, theologians should consider this school of thought suspect. Also, when looking at the teachings of the Apostolic Fathers, we may consider how close Paul is quoted in relationship to his views of the resurrection. An Apostolic Father is someone that succeeded and was taught by an Apostle. Many believe *The Parable of the Ten Virgins* was taught so that people would not give up on following Jesus as the second resurrection hadn't happened soon enough. It was taught by the Pharisees that when the Messiah came and established the Kingdom, there would soon be a resurrection. This may have confused many of the Jewish Christians, as did the issue of what the Gentiles were to follow concerning this new Jewish faith. But with Paul being the author of most of the Christian text, he would have internalized his understanding of Jewish tradition and expressed it in his writings.

The twenty-seven Gospels and letters preserved by the early church accumulated much earlier than scholars would like to admit. With as many facts as possible, various views have been hypothesized. It would seem that the last two books to be added to the total would have been Revelation and Jude: Revelation as it was the book from the last surviving Apostle, and Jude as he was Jesus' brother. The last three books before Revelation and Jude would have been the Gospel of John, Luke and Acts. The Gospel of John has its ties to John and Gnostic text, and Luke and Acts were written to Ignatius, for he was an important individual that Luke addresses the stories to by his Christian title.

Understanding that the stories were told for one reason and have only one interpretation prompts the true seeker to study them with a critical mind. The meaning of the story should be understood as what the audience should have been learning. Everyone cannot come up with a different interpretation and think that every teaching is correct. This pluralism is absurd even though it can be interesting. But Jesus told a parable to the crowds in order that the crowd might see the errors of their religious teachings. These parables were antireligious as Jesus had to contend with the religious leaders' false teachings. Jesus would question their religious thinking in order to teach them some ethical value. Parables are not only stories of ethical values that contradicted religious teachings, but also develop an antireligious theme that is subjective. The contention between Jesus and religion is what causes the anti-religion in the parables. These are two things to consider when comprehending what Jesus meant. Therefore, only a critical mind can really see the impact of what Jesus was teaching.

THE ETHICAL

The ethical is much easier to perceive than the antireligious. That a Parable is a story with an ethical meaning and an antireligious theme is knowledge deeply imbedded in the audience's prior understanding. Morals are the realization of ethics. The ethical in *The Ten Virgins* consists of multiple ethical views. It is hard to figure out the exact view that Jesus was trying to teach the disciples, audience and Pharisees. The years between then and now have produced distortion in our understanding of the correct purpose of the teaching. One teaching could be that there is a right and wrong way to get things done. The foolish virgins went wandering at the wrong time. They didn't follow the orders that were given them. Many people do not follow the Bible, but make up their own ideas and interpret the Bible in light of those beliefs. In fact, we all do that within our human condition. The problem starts subjectively when we condemn others for incorrectly interpreting the Bible and perceive them as promoting those ideas that are not founded on what the Biblical authors were trying to teach. By this act we condemn ourselves, for we are all blind and guilty of practicing the same act of misinterpreting the Bible. Individuals realize this when they say their doctrine is the only correct belief, or their church is the only one that is doing and believing the right things. If we do this we leave the ethical behind as we create our own antireligious theme while interpreting text to our own advantage.

A second understanding of the ethical is closely related to the first example. It is when one continually looks for more light. The realized knowledge is not enough and the ethical is put into suspension until the right truth is found. This is when we turn Christianity into a religion instead of a relationship. Many today claim that Christianity is a relationship as taught by Barth, but still insist that others should follow a proven doctrine. Whenever a term associated or interpreted as doctrine is mentioned in the Christian text it mostly precedes a reference to caring for others or mentions the fruit of the Spirit. There doesn't seem to be an outline in the Christian text of what dogmatic views to hold, but the text seems to bring into light those things that are helpful to the self in order to build up the body of Christ. The foolish virgins were looking for more oil, as they should have kept their eyes on Jesus. But for some, Jesus is not the example, but only the distant Savior. Even if you only have a little light, keeping your eyes on the ethical is the same as seeing Jesus as the example to follow. When realizing the ethical by continually reading the Bible, you will find your life changing. The more oil that you will find by reading and understanding the Biblical text, the more God will produce the correct Spirit within you.

The last idea I wish to mention, although there are many more, teaches that truth is subjective. This doesn't mean that each of us has our own truth, but that concrete truth can only be found within an individual. Although there is objective truth, subjective truth is what every individual seeks in order to find peace. Subjective truth is the reflection of the objective world. Although all of the bridesmaids were virgins, some did not really have what was needed subjectively. Some had it in them to bring more oil. The oil could represent many things. But it is the self that makes choices, and whether or not you have Christ in you, your choices reflect the truth that is in you. Jesus in his lessons first tried to convince others to think differently and not to act differently. Acting differently will result when you think differently. When the Spirit comes on individuals, they act differently if they let the Spirit lead them. This leading is not some objective place, but a subjective change in one's life. We can all make ourselves look acceptable to others living in whatever community we decide to reside in, yet we can only change with the accepting of what God gives us, without complaining that it isn't as we expected. Paul had to write many letters to the churches because of the objective things individuals were expecting in Christianity. The reason why those letters are so relevant is that today we suffer from the same human condition of accepting the outward appearance. This inward relational change is Christianity, in opposition to some creed or building. The church manifests itself when individuals are built up through and by each other in realizing this change through meditation on the Biblical text. This building up by the actions of each member of the body is done through subjective molding that is realized by the power of God and not some outward manifestation of a creed or intellectual concept. Creeds and intellectual concepts can only point to some subjective relationship with Christ and not replace it.

THE ANTIRELIGIOUS

The enlightenment of the antireligious teaching woven into this parable is needed in order to understand the correct meaning of the text. Some commentators express this viewpoint even though they don't refer to it as an antireligious theme. It seems that most parables have or seem to have some type of antireligious connection. And the *Ten Virgins* is not an exception from those that have antireligious themes. The *Parable of the Talent* also produces an antireligious tone, but this tone is somewhat latent in expressing this connotation until we learn that these two parables address the same issue. We should realize that just because we are religious does not mean we are known by Christ. The audience's Biblical upbringing created the foundation for this antireligious theme that is found throughout the parables.

Many teachings refer to this parable as alluding to the rapture and being ready. But during the resurrection it doesn't matter where you are, but rather what Christ has made you. This would lead to the ethic that reveals there is little difference between that and the antireligious meaning of the text. Depending on how you understand a parable will cause you to see what depth of antireligious theme the parable holds. In this respect parables can produce some type of different application as everyone uniquely interprets their experiences. Although a parable really has only one meaning, we can realize the story in our life differently, but the ethical and antireligious meaning remains absolute. This is why even though the parable may not be about the rapture, we can always find meaning to the text in reference to our preconceived ideas.

Although most people see the story known as *The Parable of the Ten Virgins* as addressing an issue about the time Christ will call saints to be with him, and this would be in context of what Christ was addressing, but we should understand that this story is more than warning us to be ready. We must also understand what it means to be ready. The story's didactic quality shows that just because one is symbolically a virgin doesn't mean the groom accepts that virginity. That is, if the virgin does represents us symbolically in our religious state. God did not accept Cain's sacrifice. Whether we understand the virgins as being unspotted from the world or the bridesmaids, the symbolism changes little. The wise virgins would be the true Christians and the foolish virgins would be the false Christians. The bridegroom would be Christ. There are many different understandings of what the oil represents. Some believe it is the spirit of an individual and others believe it represents the Holy Spirit. And even others believe the second container of oil is the Holy Spirit and that is what the foolish virgins were missing. Other parables will bring out the correct understanding as we comprehend what Jesus taught.

"That is why we rationalize that we are correct in most of our thinking and Biblical interpretation."

The virgins didn't need much oil for the ritual and this is easily understood if you know the Jewish tradition. These foolish virgins seem to be led by their own understanding and went looking for more of the Spirit instead of accepting what they had. Too many look for more than just grace to save them. They look for that which will make them perfect, so that they can show that they have been saved by their works of knowledge. Yet knowledge that is believed to save you is in many respects works, if you believe that knowledge or acting on knowledge is needed by everyone to have a closer walk with God or obtain salvation. This knowledge is works if you believe by doing or following a ritual or believing something beyond faith saves you from God's wrath. The only oil is in the Bible and can produce workable light by letting the text change you naturally and through the Spirit and not some intellectual understanding.

PARABLE OF THE TALENTS

In this same sense of the last ethical manner, in *The Parable of the Talents* one of the servants was condemned by the master as the wicked servant. This servant believed that the master was cruel, so that servant did nothing to increase the talent given him. It should be noted that the Master gave talents to each of the servants, although not equally. The other servants did not believe the master to be cruel, and increased their talents in proportion to what they were given. If you are wicked, you will believe God is wicked and therefore you will not be able to receive much from God. The subjective-self of the wicked servant reflected his own personality onto the master and thereby saw the master as evil. Many of us comprehend the creator as being much like ourselves. That is why we rationalize that we are correct in most of our thinking and Biblical interpretation. But this self-correct viewpoint will lead many in the wrong direction by leaning on their own understanding instead of following Christ. The wicked servant, concerning himself, fell into this self-correct opinion due to his objective understanding of existence.

It is absurd to think that the talents are something that we can do well and should use for religious means. Talents are the measure of the Spirit that we are able to accept from God. This story cannot be teaching about each person's individual worldly talents. The absurd interpretation that the money would be symbolically referring to our abilities loses the total definition of the story, as it refers to a different type of ability. Yet this symbolic interpretation is taught and accepted by many Christians, and blinds us from the true understanding of the parable. The talents are the measure of the Spirit that you are given. As you grow in the Spirit and let it lead your life; you will produce more fruit. These talents must represent the Holy Spirit as that is what God gives us so that we can grow.

STORIES ARE TEACHING THE SAME THING

And the wicked servant in the parable of the talents could have put his money in the bank making interest, but didn't consider this option due to his fear of the master. These stories (Talents & Virgins) are both examples of the fruit in someone's life, in that both acted out of their will and believed their acts were correct even though it was fear that motivated them. If we are children of God, we should not fear God because of God's nature. Biblical fear is respect toward that which should be worshipped. These individuals condemn themselves just as God doesn't condemn any, but judges them according to their own existential knowledge. So it is the individual that condemns the self and his or her fruit will be what God and saint can see in order to judge.

Furthermore, a deeper investigative search into these two stories reveals that the ones found lacking believed in the return of someone important, yet didn't really accept that they would be accepted, or else they would have never acted as they did. This is what is meant by a *leap-of-faith*: to believe in something that is so unacceptable, except that God said it was true, even though it is beyond our rational understanding. A leap is not something you presumptuously believe. How can we refute this train of thought while examining our personal sin? Only those that look outwardly and not inwardly deny this absurd truth. The foolish virgins believed they needed more and instead of waiting, they decided to go and maybe buy what they needed so that the bridegroom would be pleased. The foolish servant was afraid of his master, so he did nothing. His very belief in the master's personality, although incorrect, caused him to fear. In both cases they did not accept the true nature of the one that was important.

So many of us are like the foolish virgins and in order to get more of the Spirit we look for the right dogma. Or like the foolish servant, we are too afraid to do anything as we want not to sin and make the master mad. Both have an attitude about what is needed. Just as the virgins had to look for more oil, with the right dogma many times we believe we may get more of the Spirit by following some train of thought. It is commonly accepted that the oil represents the Spirit, yet why were the foolish virgins looking for more of the Spirit? Was it because they were not prepared? Maybe something much deeper was at work, such as that they didn't believe they were prepared? Many today run for more of the Spirit.

"Nothing we can do can complete our salvation and make ourselves more acceptable in God's eyes."

So the foolish servant hid his talent as he believed the master would be mad, or he did nothing because he believed the master to be evil. Both the virgins and the servant did not see the one that they were honoring in the true light of what that one person was, as fear gripped them and they did what they thought would make them right in the sight of the one that is symbolic of God or right in their own self-centeredness. These characters wanted to trust in their own ways to get favor, but were mistaken in that knowledge. They could not accept the gift as being a gift, as they didn't trust the one that was calling them. This is a true reflection of human nature.

If being a virgin is a symbolic representation of being religious and unspotted from the world in this parable, one can see an antireligious meaning. The two types of handmaidens were virgins, so that both types are similar and this similarity may be that they were religious, but one type of virgin lacks that which only the Spirit could give, and that is to accept the grace of God. When one understands the tradition of the handmaidens, then it is easy to comprehend that the virgins should not have left the house to go buy oil. The foolish virgins only needed the oil for a little while and their job was to welcome the one that was coming. Nothing we can do can complete our salvation and make us more acceptable in God's eyes. Paul put all his knowledge away to know Christ. He knew Christ not by religious or any other knowledge, but only by experience. When Paul strived to be more like Christ, it was neither by wearing some clothes, nor participating in a religious tradition, nor by some theological understanding, but by living the compassion of Christ. Even though Paul asked for books to be sent to him, he did not rely merely on knowledge.

The servant also was given something from the master, which is a type of God's gift for each one of us. But the servant was foolish in his thoughts toward the master; in the same respect we can misunderstand the love of God and find ourselves worrying more about not sinning, or not doing wrong to keep God's acceptance. The action of the servant hiding his talent could be compared to Christians trying to be righteous through their religious life, and thereby missing the mark of what God wanted. In this respect it is a sin to hide our true nature by convincing others of our false holiness.

The love of knowledge that lifts one up is the root of all religious evil. To believe that someone has some understanding that will guide you from a situation where you are not children of God to a position where you are thought of as being accepted by God is one of the reasons that many cannot find salvation. Salvation comes through experience, not some understanding that has to be sought out. The knowledge in the Bible is all we need. This experience can only come from God. There is a difference between the experience and the knowledge of the experience. Maybe God uses this disjointedness to blind those that do not have a relationship with him, so that they may continue in their acceptance of those beliefs that do not center on a relationship with God. When we believe we must find the right teacher to understand salvation correctly, we are attempting to know God without the experience and Biblical knowledge. We want to rely on our own knowledge to find salvation. This is a type of works. Works is trying to do things in order to merit salvations, but behind any type of work is knowledge without experience. For instance, we may know that it is a

Christian virtue to feed the poor. So if we feed the poor, we may have an experience and believe the self to be better in the sight of God through the experience. This is an example of knowledge that does not save. But when we experience the compassion of God, we will feed the poor, as our being has been changed with compassion for the poor. Yet even the understanding of this compassion is different from the experience of the compassion.

So the story about the Ten Virgins was probably better understood by those that were hearing the parable for the first time, as the story would be part of their Jewish tradition. They would understand the story and the implications of what Jesus was trying to show them. The question remains, what is so important about the figures and what did they mean to the Jewish people that were hearing the story? Today we have become so far removed from the Jewish roots that we cannot even accept many of the correct understandings because we refuse to learn the Jewish train of thought and what certain ceremonies meant in their daily existence. Many of these parables originated from cultural traditions like our national holidays, yet more troubling is that we do not see those Biblical Jewish traditions as national concepts, but as religious rites.

It should be understood that not much oil was needed, yet the foolish virgins left their place and went to look for more oil. They were foolish because they left. And the act was one of disobedience to what they were supposed to do. Many Christians today run to look for what will give them more oil in their walk with God and by doing so lose out and will find themselves not known by Christ. It is not an outward search but an inward removal of the self that brings us closer to God. It is no mystery to be like the wise virgins and the ones that increased their talents. A change of heart is the repentance that God desires. The search is subjective and not objective and every Jewish listener would have understood this parable in this light.

When we look everywhere for more of Christ, such looking is not the answer, for we look through a glass darkly. Every dogmatic and systematic theology is foolishness to God, as our righteousness is comparable to filthy rags. Religion is vanity. It is often merely how good one can make the self look to others. But religion is nothing without the blood or even with the blood if one accepts one's true nature. The heart is continuously wicked, but the religious part of one's being will tell the self that God looks at the heart. If this were true, God could easily change one's heart to the point that the churches would be full of Christ-like people. But everyone fails daily as the heart and knowledge deceives the self. It is true the heart takes part in salvation, but it is not because of our heart, but in spite of our heart that God chooses us. This choice will remain a mystery.

CHAPTER 4
ETHICAL AND ANTIRELIGIOUS VIEWS

Being religious means asking passionately the question of the meaning of our existence and being willing to receive answers, even if the answers hurt.

Paul Tillich (The Lost Dimension In Religion)

And in vain they worship Me, teaching as doctrines the commandments of men.

Matthew 15:9 (The Bible—New International Version)

Rarely do we find men who willingly engage in hard, solid thinking. There is an almost universal quest for easy answers and half-baked solutions. Nothing pains some people more than having to think.

Martin Luther King Jr. (Strength to Love)

PERSONAL SALVATION

When Carl Barth proclaimed that *Christianity was a relationship and not a religion*, the statement immediately became less than pragmatic. The reason is wherever you see Christianity, you witness religious organizations that develop from those that claim Christianity as their faith. Also the statement is not clear even though many understand it in the content of their belief system. Throughout history writers have taught a division within Christianity by using such terms as Kierkegaard's *church of the Bible* versus *church of Christendom,* or the visible versus the invisible church, or some other dichotomy to explain this rationalization even before the birth of Barth. Seemly, what Barth implied was already realized in other Christian philosophies and by theologians before Barth's parents were conceived. Barth simply verbalized the concept in a more personal, expressive way so that outward religious Christianity pointed to a more subjective Christianity.

"Those that argue against a personal relationship with Christ do not have this relationship and therefore they denounce it as a fraud."

Barth's notion came from the ethical and antireligious problems that have always plagued Christianity. When reading the story known as *The Parable of the Weeds*, you can understand the implications of any teaching that affirms a division between real and false Christians. Mutual fellowship is suspect and cannot be correct when thinking about the dynamics of the body of Christ. Jesus gives the interpretation that seems to claim one church in the realization that Jesus said let the wheat and weeds grow together. So even if Bath's statement contains any pragmatic hope, it may be less than that when looking into the different meanings that have evolved from the phrase. The statement does contain an interdenominational approach to the body of Christ. That phrase is also connected with a modern day expression where Jesus Christ is proclaimed as a personal savior, for they are both existential statements. Without understanding the connection between these two phrases the true meaning cannot be realized. This contention about Barth's statement is probably spawned through those that argue against a personal relationship with Christ. In their experience no such relationship exists, therefore they denounce it as a fraud. Of course, it would be foolish to affirm something that you have never experienced and which only exists through a relationship with God and the subjective self.

One way of interpreting the statement is to believe that Jesus is someone you can talk to as a friend. Jesus is easy to approach and walks with you everywhere you go and speaks to you as you speak to him. This is a new way of praying which is more personal than just falling on your knees and bowing before a great and mysterious being in the right place at the right time. Some would claim that this statement means that religion is personal and that having a relationship God means that they do not need to share it with others. Others will say that this personal relationship is something they must share. The former people say that they do not need to attend church services, for all the organizations are corrupt and those that attend are usually hypocrites. These people do not care for organized religion and avoid it at all cost, believing they are doing what God expects. Others will explain that Christianity is something you must do for yourself and that you cannot be a Christian just because your parents are or you were raised in a Christian nation. So "personal" here means a personal commitment to one's religion. And then others oppose that statement as being unbiblical. They stress that this statement is not found in the Christian writings and that Christ chooses us and not the other way around. One group stresses that it is a personal commitment by oneself to Christianity and not a relationship with a church or Christ. Then there are those that claim that religion and relationship are not mutually exclusive, therefore the statement is suspect. In this respect God demands both relationship and religion or the religion is empty and without meaning. What Barth meant was probably that Christianity must be a subjective act and not just an outward religious observance.

MORE THAN SYMBOLIC

Understanding this parable is much easier since Jesus gives the symbolic interpretation to the disciples. But the symbolic understanding was not to promote some dogmatic view of heaven and hell. This understanding was to directly influence the disciples in order to help them change their point of view about how they see the world in regard to their Jewish inheritance, and to teach others in the audience that had not hardened their hearts and would let God reveal to them the meaning. Disciples had to leave much of their previous understanding behind them as they learned the truth about the kingdom of God. So leaving the interpretation and not comprehending more of the impact of the story would be a mistake. There is still more to learn from this parable than just the given interpretation. There is an ethical value and antireligious tone imbedded in this parable. The ethical value is that if one commits sin and evil that they are not the children of the Son of Man. It is easy to see that the Son of Man is Jesus.

So what is sin and evil? These words are used often but with different meanings as everyone has a different point of view. But these points of view, although relative, are based on knowledge that is concrete which can be realized only through one's being, for this knowledge is subjective. Evil is understood as those things that are not equally judged. That is why the contrast between God's and the devil's judgment is the same as the contrast between judgment that is just and judgment that is unbalanced. A simple synonym of evil is iniquity, which means uneven. We all make judgment calls that are uneven where we apply one standard to others or a group, but refuse to apply that standard to our group or ourselves. An example is when a church organization claims they have the truth and can point out all the errors of the doctrines of others' Biblical belief systems, yet refuse to see their own errors. Or when an individual condemns someone for their Biblical interpretation while not realizing that their own understanding is flawed. We are all blind to this human condition, for we understand the world subjectively by rationalizing our experiences. No wonder Jesus called us evil. Critical thinking is not judging another belief system, but a true consideration of the errors of our own standard of belief.

Sin is a hot word with a negative connotation, yet with a simple meaning. People do not like the word's implication, and will automatically become defensive and offensive at the same time, directing their attacks against you if you use this word. What is sin? Sin is transgressing against others, God and self. We can also sin against someone and God at the same time with one act. Sin is the transgression of the laws of Moses. Depravity points to sin in the way we think. This depravation is a symptom of sin and not sin itself. We are all born into a sinful society, shaped by what we see and learn as we age with sin all around. Non-religious and religious people do not understand that when you treat someone disrespectfully, it is hard to accept that you wouldn't treat God in the same manner, as you can see a person, but you can't see God. If God stood before us as a man, how would we treat him? Probably like we treat others should be the answer. The reason why sin is used in this parable is because it is not merely ordinances or rules that the Bible wants us not to transgress, but that we should show love to one another. The Torah was written by a Spirit and meant to be spiritual. This story of the law and of love is what the Spirit was promoting. All laws, no matter what type, point to manifesting love not only outwardly but in one's spirit or what could be call subjectively as in one's complete being.

The antireligious theme is embedded in the understanding that no matter what sect of Christianity we are involved in, our systematic theology is imperfect, and contains incorrect interpretations of what it means to be Christian. Also, within any organization there are those that by nature are filled with iniquity and justify their self-centeredness in most anything they do or say. The view that while Jesus explained the field was symbolic of the world and therefore cannot be the church is latently mistaken as we cannot imagine that organizations are not filled with people that do not understand Christianity correctly. Or that this idea of the world being everyone means that those that participate in church activities are immune from the consequences of their inequalities. The phrase Kingdom of God is referring to those things that happen in the church, and the field is where Jesus sows the seed through the church. The misunderstanding that if we have the right dogmatic viewpoint we will be accepted by Christ leaves behind the grace that we receive through the blood of Jesus Christ. It should be shameful to rely on systematic theology and leave behind the mercy that flows from the cross that we should have been taught to share.

"This desire of iniquity is in all of us and we have to fight it every day."

POLITICAL MESSIAH

Jesus' use of the Kingdom of God can be viewed as antireligious, as the religious teaching of those days promoted that a political Messiah would come and free them from bondage much like Moses and others had throughout Biblical history. No wonder the first Gospel promotes Jesus as the new Moses. When Jesus refers to the Kingdom as something other than the present condition of the Jewish nation, Jesus is going against all that is being taught about the Messiah. This concept of the Kingdom of God is so subversive that many do not or cannot explain the implications that this phrase had as it dynamically impacted the Jewish listeners of Jesus' audience. Christians latent rejection of the Jewish writings produces this lose of understanding of the Kingdom of God, as modern Christians rely mostly on the Christian text to understand their lives.

Why are there so many churches? Which church is THE church? Since Jesus used the word 'World,' many say this parable is not referencing the Church. But it is Jesus that sows the seed through his body. That is why when we read the phrase, "while everyone was sleeping," many accept it as referring to the saints. Sleeping simply means that while they were not watching, as many of us are not spiritual enough to know the difference between wheat and tares. We are what make the body weak, not Christ. As both wheat and tares grow, they must grow in the church. Wherever we go, we sow seeds, for even our lives produce seeds as we are epistles read by the world.

Although we are still sinful, the Blood of Christ hides our sins from others for His glory, not to make us look religious. When the tares grow to adulthood they can be cast out of the body of Christ, for then they are adult enough to be seen by their fruits. But while the tares are young they need to grow alongside the wheat, as we cannot look into someone's heart and tell if they are a tare or wheat. You cannot tell if someone is going to develop good fruit or thistles until they are completely mature. One verse that is so misrepresented explains how to remove tares but has been interpreted to mean that any time people are together praying, Jesus is there with them.

"Even though we would wish to do good, our self-centeredness is always present."

In this parable if Jesus were speaking of the world without reference to the church, we would have a type of Zoroastrianism. This parable would teach that good people go to heaven and bad people go to hell. Of course this is completely absurd, for we are all evil. The body of Christ sows the seed in the world, which is the church. We only grow in the fruit of the Spirit as God changes us, not because we will it ourselves. We cannot will to be good even though we try, we will fail in the end. The field is the world but those that sow the seed do it through the Son of Man, that is, Christ working though the Holy Spirit. The law could not make anyone better as it had no conversion quality. That may be one reason the Jewish philosophies did not teach evangelize, as their tradition believes salvation comes from inheritance. Biblical laws only show us that we are evil. Subjectively, if we look inward and understand our own state of being, we would admit that even though we would wish to do well, our self-centeredness is always present.

Some teach that Zoroastrianism influenced Judaism and others teach that Judaism influenced Zoroastrianism. Of course both sides of the disagreement are speculating and at best it will never be resolved. Neither Judaism nor Christianity meant to teach that good people go to heaven and bad people go to hell. But this could have been derived from the text just as the inference of the opposite could have been imposed onto the Bible.

The *Torah* pointed to the moral ways of living, but leaders put more emphasis on the rituals and following guide lines, for they were teaching what they thought was pleasing and wanted by God. How much more do Christians reflect this same attitude? Israel believed that since they were the children of Abraham, God had chosen them to lead the world through, not to, the Messiah. They believed that their Messiah would subdue all nations and Israel would rule forever. Unfortunately, the truth was something different for Israel and the Gentile nations. More is expected from the Gentiles than just following the correct nation, yet one day Israel will rule.

RACIST VIEWS

Some claim that this parable addresses an issue on the division of Judaism and Christianity. But the symbolisms used cannot be correct for the planter first sowed the good seed and then later the Devil sowed the bad seed. So we would have to strain to put that kind of interpretation systematically into this story. Also, this concept is far from any teaching by Jesus and Paul, as they reflect the opposite of everything this school of thought teaches. Christianity came from Judaism, not Judaism from

Christianity, and it would not deny its own teachings. Christianity could not come into existence without Judaism. Christians understand moral implications and sin through the Torah and the history of the Bible. Christianity became grafted in by the work of Christ. No matter how large the grafted branch becomes, it doesn't become the trunk. The grafted section is not Christianity, but Jesus. A sect of Christians that follows philosophers or theologians in order to understand ethics, instead of learning from the Torah, reveals its detached racism through its disciplines, as they refuse to use the Bible as a ground of understanding.

God founded Judaism before the church, so if the first is good seed and the last evil seed, that would imply that Judaism refers to the good seed and Christianity consists of the evil seed. But human nature changes the meaning of a story for those that have new ways to believe and are looking for followers that also believe no matter how absurd the interpretation. Even though these prejudiced beliefs are accepted by many Christians, even if not verbally, but in practice, that doesn't make the interpretations correct.

Within our being, the totality of what we are as we exist, without even knowing we can judge individuals that are not like us, and can also unknowingly have accepted prejudices, for we are all blind to our true selves. Just the fact that there are racist Christians and Christian sects' reveals that anyone can claim to be Christian, and base their beliefs on their own interpretations of the Bible. Unfortunately, many say that they believe the Bible, but in fact they only believe their own understanding of what they believe the Bible means; others do not try to interpret it as they know their philosophy will not live up to a Biblical standard. The Bible's main doctrine is love, which is contrary to the individual who is a race-hater. It seems as though almost all Christians claim to base their belief on the Bible, but really justify their interpretation by using passages that seem to line up with their belief system. That is why every sect seems to have a systematic doctrine. All these types of Christianity must denounce the roots of Judaism before their organizations flourish; this proves how far from the truth they are willing to go to promote their thinking.

Although very little of Christianity seems to have accepted concepts from Judaism, except the moral teachings as recorded in the Christian text, the Jewish women and men that accepted the resurrection of Jesus as the fulfillment of the work from God through the Messiah are those Jewish people that are the foundation of the Christian church. The Christian text when referring to dogma most always mentions treating others in some form of love. The shame of the Church today is that there are so many churches, and if this story is representing the church as the Kingdom of God, then there should only be one church; all that have established a separate organization are in error by the interpretation of the concluding moral of the story. The moral of the story is to let all grow together and this is accomplished through the opposite of racism—love.

Yet the church today is divided between racial and economic classes, and this division can spawn some difficult questions that should be answered. Are there really any true Christians in the world today when there are homeless people in the same area that there are wealthy individuals that claim to be Christian? There will always be needy people everywhere as long as we live in a corrupt society that is founded and controlled by humanity; although there are many Christians working to help the poor, it is a shame when considering the modest amount that most Christians invest in charity. Revival will never take place while Christians are content to argue with doctrine and creed in hand, instead of going to the streets and feeding the poor and helping the needy. As long as there are those that are not really wanted in the church because of their status in life or educational background or even the way they talk, the church will stay blind to what its mission should be in the world. Church is not just the people in a building, but the church needs to go into the field as the Parable of the Weeds proclaims and sow good seed by action through the way they live and confess.

CHURCH TRADITION

There are parables that are not considered by the so-called educated elite as being the words of Jesus. They believe that some parables were developed by those that wanted to keep the traditions of the Church alive, as Jesus had not returned as fast as some believed He would, due to doctrines handed down from the Pharisees and some Christians' confusion concerning the resurrection. These teachings still had some strength in the church even in Paul's time. There were many confusing teachings about the resurrection. The Weeds is just one of those parables as it is not accepted by the modern intellectuals. They don't believe that Jesus had such a clear understanding of the faults of the Church, but the correct understanding of the parables will contradict any claim that Jesus didn't have full understanding of the dynamics of the body of Christ. Of course this is also absurd, as early Christian writers do not mention this story being one that was created for an explanation dealing with the character of the church. Jesus was driving home the point that you need to have moral attitudes concerning what happens in this life, for there will be a harvest when all life will be judged.

There is also a problem with taking the text out of its historical setting. Jesus was speaking to an audience and he was mostly speaking about himself and how that audience related to its historical situation; but the bottom line is that there is an existential moral teaching in the parable whether or not it is considered allegorically. Since all parables had something to do with the Kingdom of God, the relevance to hearers was to help them understand the correct meaning of the dogmatic views and the belief system that they grew up with; they were incorrect, and the parables pointed out the incorrect teachings that needed to change.

"Traditions of the Pharisees and other religious leaders caused them to worship God in vain."

The traditions of the Pharisees and other religious leaders caused them to worship God in vain. The religious leaders worshipped and followed as close as they could the written words of the Torah, even as many Jewish people do today. It is not to be understood that it is wrong to study the Torah, and we should accept that there are many Jews that do know God, as Jesus told the Samaritan lady that she didn't know who she worshipped, as do the Jews. So how much more do Christians today worship God in vain because of Christian traditions that have been handed down throughout the ages? Many confuse this with some form of denouncement of some historical belief system which by their rejection of it will bring them into the true doctrines of the first Christians. But this is absurd, even though it may have some logic behind the train of thought, that you can find out dogmatically what is needed to follow Jesus. The religious leaders and others failed to know Jesus even though these religious leaders may have believed he was the Messiah, but they didn't accept him as they couldn't see Jesus in the Bible. Unfortunately, many modern Christians cannot point out Christ in the Jewish writings.

Throughout history the argument within Christianity has been what objective knowledge is needed to clarify orthodoxy for dogmatic reasons. The true situation is that Christianity is not objective reasoning, nor is it emotional awareness, but it is subjective truth that can only be realized by knowing Christ. Objective knowledge is found in arguments about Christology as well as all other forms of traditions that have been handed down throughout history. Objective knowledge was the focus of the controversies during the Reformation, first concerning some of the practices of the Catholic Church and then later the practices and beliefs of the Protestant organizations. But parables do not deal with objective knowledge, for Jesus' stories use objective knowledge to teach subjective truth. Paul learned this after his conversion and that is why you do not find objective truth in the epistles. Truth is not some logical scientific epistemology that can be applied today to find the truth; this would be true if Christian truth was objective. Objective truth deals with many aspects of life, but cannot and will not answer the questions that everyone subjectively asks of the self. Even atheist existentialists reach out for the truth, but stop short and proclaim that life is absurd, for the only knowledge that gives life meaning is the subjective knowledge of the truth that is in Christ.

Some say they believe in God because they feel him. By this they mean that they have had emotional experiences that they believe involve God. But if someone doesn't feel

God, don't they have the same right not to believe in God because they have not realized an experience with God? With emotions we decide whether to believe or not to believe in a God, for our emotions are the vehicle that drive us to accept what logic we consider is correct in light of our experiences. The problem with emotions is that they can be based on false assumptions and deceptive knowledge. It is hard to believe that your emotions are incorrect in many situations even though the emotions are real. The parables are not based on emotion, but the understanding of the church and the subjective knowledge that follows with any relationship with Christ.

Subjective knowledge goes beyond emotion and objective knowledge. For instance, we all believe that rape is wrong. But why do we believe that it is wrong? It is something deep within a person. Despite the loneliness, anxiety and other deep emotions that cannot be changed by emotional or objective knowledge, we never-the-less find in our subjective state the ground of why we believe that rape is wrong. We can use logic and emotion to express the reason that we believe, but we also hide what we believe with the same tools. We use logic and emotion in the deep subjective self in order to survive and project what we want others to think we believe. Parables can cut through these logical and emotional walls that we put up before the world to hide the truth of what is right. But first we must disregard the traditions that blind us from their true meaning.

IMPORTANCE OF THIS PARABLE

This parable is one among many that were told that day as historically a fulfillment of prophesy. Jesus tells a couple of parables and explains the first parable without the disciples asking for an interpretation, yet the disciples did ask why he was speaking in parables. Then Jesus tells more parables but the disciples only ask him for an explanation of *The Parable of the Tares*. The disciples called this parable the parable of the weeds in the field. This gives the inference that it is the weeds that are the main topic or at least what the disciples focused on during the stories Jesus told that day. Maybe the parables should be named according to the original language or not even named at all, as words can translate from one language into more than one word in another language and then other words may not have an equivalent translation. Also this story is more precise when reading in Greek, for in English there is information lost. It explains the type of weed and maybe this is why the weeds become a very important part of the story to the disciples. Churchgoers may believe they can find both seeds in them and easily can be fooled into believing their good seed has been choked out if they promote their self-centered ambitions or see themselves not being heard by God. But this does not seem to be a good interpretation of the parable.

This story will also have many interpretations because those that are weeds are also able to interpret the parables in light of their self-promoting beliefs; it may also be interpreted by believers who are not led by the Spirit and seem to be fully grown wheat that can be harvested. But this parable was taught at the same time as other parables and all these parables point to the same concept. These parables, once understood, can be explained as one continuous thought. This thought is to grow in faith and knowledge of Christ or grow in the wisdom of this world and all that it has to offer. The parables assume, like theology, that everyone actually believes in God. These parables are important because as we grow in knowledge we can understand the truth through the proper meaning of what is the Kingdom of God. But false teachings have hidden the true meaning of what is taught in these stories.

These parables only have three subjects. The Lord Jesus, true Christians and false Christians are subjects in each of these parables. When you begin to understand these three subject matters, the meaning of the parables becomes clearer. There are many interpretations to each parable that bring up interesting concerns, but when you understand the parables, the idea of the ethical and antireligious meaning will become as bright as the sun in the middle of the summer. These three subjects are what Jesus was trying to teach about what would happen in the future church.

PROTESTANTISM: SALVATION BY RATIONALIZATION OR SALVATION BY FAITH

The Catholic Church is the only orthodox Christian organization. It is not proper to think of Protestantism as orthodox, but not all Protestants should be considered part of mainstream Protestantism. All Christian sects are children of the Catholic Church because they protest against the Holy Apostolic Roman Catholic Church. Even those that do not claim to be Protestant fill their doctrinal teachings with protest against the Catholic Church. In fact, you could probably consider that those sects that are not mainstream Protestant protest more against the teachings of the Catholic Church than those churches thought of as being within the group of mainstream Protestantism. This train of thought would fit well with these parables taught by Jesus that day. Protestantism believes that you participate in Christian life because you are saved while Catholicism believes that participating is what saves you.

Most of these organizations that do not believe they are Protestants claim that the Catholic Church is the mother church recorded in the prophecy of the Christian text. Furthermore they claim that the protestant churches are the children of the woman that sat on the beast. Of course they do this ignorantly, as they do not understand the definition of what it means to be Protestant. They thereby condemn themselves by being blind to what they actually represent. They condemn all other protestant churches because they are children of the Catholic Church while not realizing that they are in fact protestants themselves. All the teachings of these non-mainstream protestant groups are mostly based on everything they do not accept and contend against the Catholic Church. But at the same time there are many of the doctrines handed down through tradition that are accepted in one form or the other. Without a doubt in such organizations those people's whole being is understood in the light of what it is to be Catholic.

But both sides of the teachings are flawed, as you cannot rationalize or systemize the truth that is existential. You can only walk in the truth. For this reason organizational sects always blind those that believe through teaching that if they follow some creed or belief system they will inherit eternal life. This is also what was wrong with those religious leaders in the time of Jesus. It is the human condition to worship a position instead of being self-healed through a relationship. The older an organization becomes, the more it reflects those it contended with, for a new standard is created that is a synthesis of the old and the new belief system, building some of its foundation on the doctrine it contended was in error.

The reason why the old and new are not used in these writings is because God has not forgotten the promises to his people. Dividing the Bible into old and new creates a kind of anti-Semitic view in Christianity. Someday Jesus will return and fight for the Jewish nation, as he has never forsaken Israel, as some would have us believe. So the words Bible and Christian text are used. Again in Jesus' time the religious leaders taught what was to happen in the future and used logical philosophy and religious ideas to explain how everything would take place. The problem is their teachings didn't take place the way they taught because they were wrong. This is one reason that the disciples, crowds and religious leaders did not understand what Jesus was saying; their unbelief came from the confusion that was generated through incorrect teaching that was imbedded in them since they were young, being taught by the renown leaders. They were looking for a Messiah that would free them in his lifetime, but instead they were given one that was a sacrifice for not only them but also the whole world. This sacrifice was problematic because they were not looking to see humanity saved, but only their nation.

Today it is no different. The apple has not fallen far from the tree of humanity. There are many organizations and individuals teaching their own type of eschatological viewpoint just as were those religious leaders in Jesus' time. So with all of us knowing what the end will be like, maybe everyone is wrong and we will be blind like those taught by the Pharisees. Maybe just like in Jesus' time many will not believe it as it happens because it is not going according to what they have been taught. Too many of us have just accepted what we are told is right and wrong not only in regard to what others believe but also in how we understand the Bible. If you went back before the time Jesus began his ministry and would tell others that their teachings were wrong, how many people would believe you or write you off as a radical, deluded individual? Yet there was one that did go before Jesus, and many after their conversion to Christianity still understood the Bible in light of what they had been taught by the religious leaders. The end of the age is introduced so that we can understand that we do not have a second chance before our own death.

CHAPTER 5
WEDDING BANQUET

But they and our fathers acted proudly, hardened their necks, and did not heed Your commandments.

Nehemiah: 9:16 (The Bible—New International Version)

A great many people think they are thinking when they are merely rearranging their prejudices.

William James

(Essays: The Varieties of Religiious Expereince/ Pragmatism/ A Pluralistic Universe/ The Meaning of Truth/ Some Problems of Philosophy)

JESUS WAS NOT ANTI-SEMITIC

When Jesus referred to the church, he sometimes evoked the phrase *Kingdom of God*. But when the *Parable of the Vineyard* was told he did not use these words, as the predicate of the topic discussed did not involve the Church. The Pharisees, in fact, understood that Jesus was speaking negatively concerning their spiritual condition. The parables Jesus told were to bring the

Pharisees to a point of understanding his redemptive place in the world, even if it meant that many Pharisees would not understand until after his resurrection. Parables were not meant to condemn anyone, for God condemns no one, but individuals are self-condemning through their actions and verbal confessions. When will individuals understand that God does not condemn, but blesses? Many have used the *Parable of the Wedding Banquet* to express anti-Semitic views, but these interpretations are so far removed from what Jesus taught, that if we accept such views our walk with the Creator of the universe will not only become stagnated, but will progressively become demonic. To understand demonic, you would need to read Paul Tillich's writings. God has never left his children born from Abraham, Isaac and Jacob. If we boast and promote belief systems that alienate Jewish society, we have not studied and understood correctly, or we have only esteemed some leaderships' opinions higher than that of the true nature of the Bible. To think that the writers, being Jewish, would write anti-Semitic texts is as absurd as to see this chapter as anti-existential. Christianity cannot leave its Jewish roots, God has not turned his back on the nation of Israel and God does not condemn, he blesses.

"When will individuals understand that God does not condemn, but blesses?"

It is clear in the Christian writings that the Kingdom of God that Jesus proclaimed was at hand. This kingdom is now known as the church. The church was grafted in and when a branch is grafted in, it relies on the trunk as well as other branches to develop it and sustain it while it is part of the tree. This is no easy task. If the trunk were to die, the whole tree would die, along with the grafted branch. The grafted branch would not autonomously grow new roots, self-actualized as a self-sustaining tree. But this is what you may try to believe, as the Christianity you have been introduced to and accepted is so far removed from its Jewish foundation that the Greek wisdom, embedded in each one of us, makes this concept seem perfectly logical. It may seem that this removal from Judaism is true in some respect, as the Apostles, including Paul, gave a clear explanation of what is expected of the church. This will always be the strand that holds the grafted branch onto the tree no matter how much we try to change the meaning of what it is to be Christian. Reformers will, more than likely, try to come closer to this grafted part of the branch in order to find a closer walk with God. Most of the Jewish believes at the beginning of the church age did not choose to leave their Jewish religious roots even though they had accepted Jesus as the Messiah. The Kingdom of God, the church, was and still is about the nation of Israel.

The anti-Semitic views proclaiming that God has rejected the nation of Israel in favor of Christianity are far removed from what Jesus and Paul taught. Salvation came not only by the Jewish race, but also first to the children of Israel. How to address the Christian gentiles was a concern that was resolved between Paul and the Apostles. Yet many followers of that time must have decided they had the answer, rather than the Apostles or Paul. Jewish roots do not infer that Christianity needs to go back into bondage as to what individuals must observe in dress or rituals, because it is faith in Christ that is the foundation of Christianity. Just as Abraham had faith in God, and the individuals in the Bible had faith, we also have to walk in faith with God. The *Parable of the Wedding Banquet* is about faith.

"God-haters are the most subversive form of hate-groups because these groups can point to all other types of hatred while concealing their own agenda."

The nation of Israel is known as the Apple of God's eye. The children of Abraham, Isaac and Jacob have suffered more than any other nation from those that hate God. While the Jews kept alive the laws of God, these God-haters have attacked Israel in many different ways. God-haters are the most subversive form of hate-groups because these groups can point to all other types of hatred while concealing their own agenda. Hate language is expressed in many of the church doctrines, just as Jesus prophesied in the *Parable of the Leavened Bread*. The bread grows larger as the yeast grows, just as the church becomes larger as we accept logical belief systems that condone sin and reject Israel as God's nation. With all the racism that the Jewish nation has suffered because of its ties with God, it is meaningless to think that God would ever abandon this nation. The destruction of Jerusalem and the holocaust was not because Jews rejected Jesus, but was realized in history because the evil one still understands the Jewish place in God's worldly redemption. As Christians, we have suffered much less than Israel for serving God.

Furthermore, if God's back had been turned toward Israel, history would be much different; fewer leaders both in secular and religious life would affirm God's neglecting and rejection of the Jewish race. The world phenomenon of anti-Semitic tendencies provides evidence of Israel's favor by God. But not only will God remain with His promised people, but those that condemn them or accept belief systems that belittle the children of Israel will receive their reward for accepting or doing such acts, no matter how many people they heal, evangelize or teach when making disciples. If God had rejected his people, not only would Paul not have gone into the synagogues to seek converts, but the Apostolic leaders of Christianity of the first century would have not established the leadership of the church in Jerusalem, and Paul would have never gone to Jerusalem to meet with them to confirm that his relationship and teachings from God were orthodox.

Jesus was God here on earth and his humanity was God's humanity. Even when it came to the *woman caught in adultery*, he did not condemn anyone that watched or participated in the event. As you read the story, you can see that the audience condemned themselves. The religious leaders desired to catch him in a situation that could not be resolved so that Jesus would be under their influence, just as they were under the power of the people in the community. The religious leaders acted like they were much better than the common person, yet they showed fear and submission, as they did nothing to John the Baptist or Jesus. The parables are a warning for all to repent, whether they seem to be righteous like the rich man that asked Jesus about eternal life, or the woman caught in adultery. Even the mother of Jesus was in the upper room on the day of Pentecost. When you understand that Jesus was the humanity of God manifested, your judgment calls will change.

"We condemn ourselves because we do not meet the requirements that we lay on others."

If the religious leaders had understood Jesus, then they would have seen that they were only condemning themselves. But they did have the honor of having Jesus personally plant the seed in them, as Christian history shows that many Jewish religious leaders of Jesus' time did convert after the resurrection. This was one reason that many hated Paul and even those that were in the church fought against him, as he taught the Gentiles they did not need to follow any of the traditional laws whether moral, judicial or ceremonial. There were only some moral things that the Apostles asked the Gentiles to observe, and these are recorded in the Christian text. If Paul would have taught that the Gentiles should observe and convert to Judaism, then there would have not been so much contention. But Paul taught that all were free from the bondage of the legalism that is inherent in Judaism, and the rejection of legalism was the number one concept that drove Christian Jewish leaders to attack Paul's Christianity.

We condemn ourselves because we do not meet the requirements that we lay on others. This we do blindly because every one of us existentially understands the world without being fully self-actualized. Self-actualization occurs when you see yourself as the world sees you, not when you become the product of your desires achieving self-fulfillment. Many teach that when you are what you want to be, you have fulfilled self-actualization, but this is not the true ground of defining self-actualization. If you ask questions concerning what you think you are and how you think people perceive you and bring these questions to a number of people, you will find that people see you differently than you understand yourself. A problem arises while asking people questions you pre-answered yourself, for people will have different ideas of you. In this respect it is hard to define the self. Some answers result in total contradiction when you ask enough people that know and understand you. This confusion exists as the self lives in a paradox. Hopefully with this understanding we can see how imbalanced our judgments are in relationship to others.

Because of our human condition, we seem to be full of inequality when it comes to judging others or even judging ourselves against any standard. Within Christianity, this escalates above normal when compared to the secular. One example is the individual's acceptance and preference of Biblical translations. Most devout Christians are quick to condemn other's translations, as the translators held a biased opinion, even though this is inherent in all translation, but many refuse to accept that their favorite translation also manifests biases. A second inequity occurs when teaching against false doctrine while not realizing that our individual beliefs and understanding of the Bible contain error, for no one can know or understand the complete, perfect Biblical interpretation. A third inequity occurs when we hear someone talk in such a way as not to seem Christ-like, while within our subjective-self we harbor feelings of hate, revenge and jealousy that we are well aware of yet succeed in hiding from others. In these respects, we condemn ourselves as we do not meet the standards we set for others. Another example is when we divide the Bible into Old Testament and New Testament. That brings about a complete racist, anti-Semitic attitude. Yet when Jewish people complain about this division, Christianity is totally bewildered, as they are blind to the true implications of the statement. The New Testament is the Blood of Christ not the Christian writings. The Christian writings are no more a New Testament than the Jewish writings are the Old Testament from Moses, but the blood that Moses shed was the Covenant. This Covenant was between the Israelites and God, just as Jesus' blood is the Covenant between Christians and God.

Nietzsche was right when he wrote that *the only Christian died on the cross.* The word Christian was applied by those that were not friendly toward Christianity and most Christians would deny that they are really Christ-like. It would seem that the more we pray and trust in God, the more we feel like we are far from being as sinless as Jesus Christ. Maybe this is one reason why the leavened bread has grown so well. The leavened bread is a type of the Church with all its sins. The more we grow in Christ the more we should feel unworthy, but many people exult themselves and see some new concept that must be important for all Christians to find salvation through Christ, forgetting that this is the main problem that Paul fought against. Even in Paul's time there were those that wanted to add more to grace and faith in the blood.

THE TRUTH OF THE PARABLE

In many parables, condemnation comes when a subject fears God and therefore does not respond correctly due to a subjective belief system. It is easy for us to see others, instead of ourselves, as the subject or the brunt example of a parable. We easily interject others into parables told by Jesus, and just as those religious leaders that rejected Jesus, we do not want to place ourselves into this unpopular position. God does not condemn us, yet we condemn ourselves when we see God as a terrible avenger that proclaims and acts swiftly and without mercy. If we comprehend a God without mercy, it is because we have no mercy in the ground of our being. Some parables teach us not to fear God, as the Creator takes nothing from us that we have not freely been loaned. Here is an example why not to fear God. Let's say that you have a vehicle and loan it to someone and say you will come back when you are in need of the vehicle, explaining it could be in a hour, a day, or even years, and then one day you return and proclaim it is the time that you want your vehicle back. It should be shameful for those to condemn you for the blessing they received while in possession of your asset. You are not doing anything evil by repossessing your property, but you may easily question and condemn God for doing just this very same thing. When a baby dies or God destroys some person or nation, we with the intent to dishonor God through logic begin to state an age-old dilemma of how an existing benevolent God would do no such thing. But such logic cannot be true, as you're not evil for taking back your own possessions that you let others borrow. Questioning God is a human condition, but when it is done with malicious intent, it is not for a better understanding. It is for justifying your own hatred.

In ancient times there were many trains of thought, or maybe they should be correctly called schools of thought, that dealt with questions concerning what is truth. Calling them schools may be more appropriate because individuals that promoted the same things seem to be grouped together in regards to their teachings. Many of these schools have been lost forever. Because of Alexander the Great, we have what is now our Greek inheritance and its ways of thinking. Aristotle taught Alexander and Plato taught Aristotle and Socrates taught Plato. This is very reflective of Abraham, Isaac and Jacob, but it is Socrates, Plato and Aristotle. Through these writings we find our concepts of government and other views concerning life. We have combined both trains of thought to the point that they seem one, as we even believe that the Christian writers were influenced by both. Many of these concepts we believe in today were considered impractical at that time and many ways of living have only recently been realized by humanity. There are many other schools that have been popularized because of their association with Socrates. These writings that have been saved are considered important for one reason or another. The most important reason to study these teachings that have been handed down throughout the ages is to understand how they affect us today. To be blind to this is to be blind to many Biblical concepts in their original meaning.

Since it is the historians from the victors whose opinions are most likely saved in history, there is always a bias in how history is written. It is impossible not to be biased in our interpretations concerning things that deal with existence, but through studying we can comprehend our own short-sightedness. Our viewpoints would more than likely be very different if Aristotle had never taught Alexander. We may have never known about these men's works, as they may have been lost to history. Even Christianity will give you a biased opinion if you let the Spirit open your eyes to the true teachings of the Bible as this bias is true existentialism. The authenticity of the Bible and Jesus' parables can be understood within three concepts. The first is the honesty of the Jewish historians, the second is the accuracy of Jesus' explanation of the church, and the third is the human condition that can only be explained through the ground of being.

FIRST AUTHENTICITY

First, the Bible is a different book. It is taught that the victors write history. The slant that is given by the victors is perceived as truth, and why those in power are portrayed as virtuous until someone more powerful rises and rewrites history. But the victor's power is not found in the Jewish history that we consider Biblical history. The Bible records the faults of those in power, and how they failed God over and over again. This is much different than how history would be re-defined if Germany had won the World Wars, or if the South had prevailed in the Civil War. It is beyond amazing when considering how many times Israel has been sent into bondage and have blamed no one except themselves, and when the Jews were delivered, the nation as a whole gave glory to God and did not rely on their own *will to power*. The parables are no different in that the message is not one of perfection, but shows that those in the church will be just as deviant when trying to follow God, and that like the Jewish religious leaders will worship God in vain as they teach their holy traditions instead of God's truths. This honest accuracy testifies to the truth that the Bible was written by holy men as the Spirit of God moved them. While it may be understood that these holy men wrote as they were in an ongoing relationship with God, the truth is they, like us, were just human.

Some point to errors of one kind or another in the Bible, but the Bible is a religious and historical document for the Jews first and then to all the rest of us that wish to know God. It does not have to live up to the God of science, the God of history or the God of logic, but only needs to speak to the ground of each one of our beings. Criticism should always be welcomed, yet those that do not have the Spirit of God cannot understand what God is trying to say to the world until they are empowered by the Spirit. Unfortunately, the powers that be are not the authority of Biblical history.

SECOND AUTHENTICITY

The second, the *Parable of the Wedding Banquet* is not a history of the Jewish nation beating and killing the prophets, thereby refusing to take part in the wedding, but since the phrase "the kingdom of God" is used, the reference is to the church. The story can be seen as how the Church emulates Israel in beating and killing God's messengers. In fact, the Jewish nation ranks low in comparison to Christendom in regard to killing their prophets and teachers. Some have said that the *church is the only army that will kill its wounded* with no regrets. Christians have done this throughout the ages while believing they have done God's will. Others have hid behind the name of Christianity. Some do such acts believing they were immune, even though these acts deny God's existence. Just as the Jewish religious leaders rejected Jesus, Christians many times reject Jesus' calling. It is often said that a person here or there acts like a Pharisee, and not only is this more true than what we wish to believe, but Jesus taught this was going to happen through many of his parables.

THIRD AUTHENTICITY

The third concept that shows the evidentiary credibility of the Bible is humanity itself, as it contrasts what it is to be human against what it is to be Christian. Although we are all different in many respects, in the ground of our being, we are essentially the same. We have come into the world in the same manner and in many respects in the same manner life will end. But the ground of what we are before and after being Christian is the mystery that can only be explained through theology. As William James said, *If everyone went through a true Christian conversion, the world would be a much better place to live even if the person did not observe the newfound experience in Christianity.*[2] If we take a trip through philosophy until we end with theology, we may find the ground of our existence. The problem is as we divide existence, concepts become tainted and not reflective of reality. The philosophical journey may go as follows: We first may divide existence into two parts; these two parts are called objective and subjective, although this division only exists in the mind of humanity. Objective existence is what you see and touch. You can also see yourself as an object along with others that are objects, for you cannot see their subjective selves. If God exists and the story of Jesus is true, then the only school of existentialism that is not tainted is Christian existentialism. God's existence is also assumed by theology. Theology doesn't argue the existence of God, as it presupposes the God that is exists. This God has manifested himself in the person of Jesus the Christ.

EXISTENTIAL TRUTH

Both objective and subjective self can be further divided between nature and nurture. The objective nature is all that has not been touched by humanity. The nurture is when humanity changes the environment, tames animals and creates objects like chairs and homes. Both these we can understand as things that are outside of us, but what is important is that which is within each one of us. If we trust in objective truths and desire them, we will grow in bad faith, for objects cannot keep us happy and only hide the true self. Of course, we do not like to divide things into parts, as this again distorts the true nature of existence.

The subjective self can also be divided between nature and nurture. This is harder to divide and the argument in one form or another has been around for a long time. Nature is what is normal, as in how we think. Nurture is those things that through the influence of others have changed what we are as compared to what is natural. Society can change our nature, along with many other things that happen in life. But there is something that is more transcendent in the subjective self.

This transcendence is the ground of our existence. In the very depth of our existence lies what no one other than God can change. This is what changes in us when God becomes a part of our lives. We have anguish as we are alone due to our separation from the God that exists. Because of this separation from the infinite One, we have become finite and long to be infinite. Furthermore, since we cannot will this for ourselves, our existence is grounded in anxiety that affects everyone; yet most of us hide our symptoms of anxiety. The more we look into the abyss of what we see in our deepest self, the more we realize that something exists which is greater than ourselves.

REPEATING TEACHING

There is another parable that is similar to this story of the Banquet. Although many parables are only mentioned once and Jesus more than likely told parables that did not make it into the Gospels, he also more than likely repeated many of his stories. In fact, he probably didn't tell the story exactly the same each time as he was teaching some lesson. Jesus telling the same story to different groups can latently be seen in the two parables: the *Banquet* and the *Marriage Supper*. Although the parables are very similar, they are also different. There are also the sermons of blessings where it seems that Jesus spoke while on a hill and another time after coming off of the high place. This is due to his being seen as the new law giver. Many people try to use the quality of the stories that are different to show that the Bible is in error, yet this is just an excuse for those that do not want to believe, as they wish to satisfy some self-centeredness.

FREE WILL AND PREDESTINATION

In the *Parable of the Wedding Banquet,* one individual comes without the proper garments. The popular teaching is that we should prepare for the return of Christ. But maybe this individual relied on his own righteousness instead of the righteousness in Christ. This interpretation would make the parable antireligious. This story already shows its anti-religion in the sense that the parable proclaims that those that were invited refused to attend. Those that refused to show were the righteous people on the earth. The ethical issue is that they relied on their self-righteousness and therefore believed they didn't need Christ. This antireligious view imbeds itself in the ethical. The ethical in many of the parables condemns the outward righteousness, for inward, in the subjective-self, we are all evil and workers of inequality. The evil that engulfs us manifests itself as self centeredness. Therefore our outward righteousness means nothing, as only true righteousness will cause us to accept God's invitation to the banquet.

There remain controversial discussions in regard to free will and predestination, also known as Armenianism and Calvinism. An example of free will is that you can decide to lead a horse to water, but you can't make the horse drink;

and an example of predestination would be that you cannot make a tadpole grow legs and you can't get it to jump, only God does it all. In this parable of the *Wedding Banquet* it seems like free will would win out if there were only this parable known, for the ones that were worthy decided not to come and the ones that were not worthy were asked and chose to come. Yet, the argument is imposed onto the Biblical interpretation due to traditional ties.

With this traditionally-divisional argument, both sides are absurd, as we will not understand these puzzling concepts until we are like Jesus. Free will under investigation seems absurd, as an all-powerful God could destroy everything in one clearing of a throat. Predestination finds its absurdity in that we would not deserve hell, because we have no choice whether we are saved. But both concepts must have an insight into something that is real. The true meaning of the parable is that we cannot logically figure out who is right or wrong, for it is a subjective action that leads us to Christ and leads us to the banquet.

It seems as though many would like to believe in soft determinisms or some kind of free-will fate. This is just a compromise between the two opinions and doesn't resolve the issue; therefore we may never find a resolution until the end of time when God will open our eyes. Or maybe we will learn the whole argument is absurd. Determinisms used to be thought of as fate before Christianity. The arguments between these two concepts have taken on many forms before it became an issue in theology. Those that believe we have no real free will must believe that we all have some fate awaiting us, and no matter what we have done or will do, we were destined to end up with something in our lives over which we have never had any control. Before Christianity, some believed that if we found favor with the gods, we could escape our fate. This thought is embedded in Christianity, except Christianity uses different philosophical concepts to achieve essentially the same end.

Some sects within Christianity teach that our fate should be to end up in hell, as not only are we born separated from God, but at death we will also go to a place where we are separated from God for eternity. There is no denying that this concept may have some truth in it, yet it is not completely spelled out in the Christian text. In fact, Paul says that we cannot judge another servant's master. We all must take account of the place we hold in this world. We can only see darkly into what God desires. Paul was given a thorn in the flesh so that he would not think so highly of himself due to the exclusive knowledge that he received from God. Therefore, knowing Paul did not reveal all that he knew, we should humble ourselves realizing that all of us have a shallow understanding of God's truths.

The issues have never completely brought out the difficulty that Calvin struggled with while trying to answer this question of God's sovereignty, as many people cling to the defense of one position or the other without every reading Calvin or those that disagreed with him. Calvin seemed to use local truth and thereby would have leaned towards determinism in his pursuit of a solution. As for those that accepted Armenianism, their thoughts would have been looking at the problem with an ontological view of what is truth. If we do not investigate a viewpoint and try to understand the falsity of our beliefs, then we really don't believe what we were taught and are only expressing some viewpoint of an individual that we esteem as more important than the Bible. Paul said leave behind those issues that cause division; since the reformation this dilemma has probably caused the most division. Many people study to solidify their belief as they find evidence after evidence that condones their position on an issue. Rather, we should be looking for the contradictions in our belief system, as that would be nobler. The parables are about moral issues, not metaphysical truth handed down by tradition, yet the later interpretation finds acceptance among most believers.

CHAPTER 6
THE WORKERS IN THE VINEYARD

These are murmurers, repiners; according to their desires walking, and their mouth doth speak great swellings, giving admiration to persons for the sake of profit;

Jude 16 (The Bible—New International Version)

Then there are the fanatical atheists whose intolerance is the same as that of the religious fanatics, and it springs from the same source...They are creatures who can't hear the music of the spheres.

Albert Einstein (The New Quotable Einstein)

It is absolutely safe to say that, if you meet somebody who claims not to believe in evolution, that person is ignorant, stupid or insane (or wicked, but I'd rather not consider that).

Richard Dawkins (Ignorance is No Crime)

CHARISMATIC LEADERS

Although alluding to the lesson, most saints do not realize this parable's important meaning. It is not enough just to know or use words of wisdom when it comes to ethical situations. It is important when trying to understand *The Parable of the Vineyard Owner* that you place it in context so that the complete writings reveal the true ethical situation of the story. In the text, individuals, because of their self-centeredness, wanted to know about their importance in God's kingdom. We can condemn them easily as we read the text, but in that situation we would more than likely think and act the same way. In fact, in the churches today many have expectations to be or participate in something that makes them look important.

The disciples and others, in the text, were not thinking or referring to their position in the church, for they had no concept that the church would emerge, even though that is what Jesus was proclaiming, but were referring to when the Messiah set up his everlasting kingdom where no one will die and the Messiah would reign forever. An overcoming Messiah is what all the disciples were expecting, because they were taught by the religious community to believe in someone that would free them from their situation as an occupied country. First, Jesus tells the rich man what he needs to do to inherit eternal life, which the rich man rejected at that time; then Jesus had to tell his followers that the first shall be last and the last first in references to positions when it comes to rewards at the time when all will receive eternal life. First being last and last being first is an important concept that is very misunderstood. Also, this concept of first being last and last being first is not realized in the church or in the individual believer's walk with God, because we are not taught the right way to think in regards to the body of Christ. After telling the parable, Jesus began to explain to them that he must die. When understood correctly this fits right into the subject.

"First being last and last being first is an important concept that is very misunderstood."

Jesus talking about his death fit perfectly with this parable, because he was without sin and should not have died. He is the head of the church, but he gave away more than any one of us can. He died even though he had not sinned, as we will die because we have all sinned. He is like those that worked in the vineyard the longest. Yet we are the ones that received something, not Jesus. Therefore, Jesus should have not died because he was sinless, and sin is what makes us finite. Sin also breaks communion with the infinite. Jesus, being sinless, washed the sinful disciple's feet and by doing this act, showed the disciples an example on how to lead, as this act of washing was an example of how they should disciple those that would follow after the resurrection. Jesus was an example of servitude in that he was in the form of God and was born as a man to serve all humans.

If we wish to be like Jesus, we should not study so that we can outsmart those in authority, or to convert someone to our way of thinking, but we must put on Christ who was a person that served. But the concept of servant has changed and the change has been accepted by too many of us that believe in Christ. We need to look deep into the Bible to see what kind of servitude is the correct way to lead. To take charge, and control those that wish to serve God is a sin within itself that denies the very essence of

God. The words server and leadership are two dynamically opposed words, but many have put these words together in order to confuse the issue. There are many leaders in the church organizations today, but not very many servants.

Jesus did not scare his followers with tactics that if they left him, they would burn in hell for eternity as many organizations do these days in order to control converts. Although he was the God of the universe, he did not say anything to force anyone to follow him. When Jesus taught hard things, many people stopped following him, but he didn't condemn any one of them, but just asked his disciples if they would leave and stop following him. In contrast, today we have many leaders that proclaim they are the only church and they are the only ones that are important because God called them and all others are lost. But we do not find this disunity in the Christian text. Or they teach that their doctrine is so important that if we follow the doctrine we will be the only true children of God and all others that claim to be saints are in fact children of Satan or lost. Both of these teachings are not found in the example that Christ or the Apostles left in their words or actions.

Doctrines of division are condemned by the very nature of the creed, for it truly changes the meaning of stories and examples in the Bible. Those that will not be controlled are condemned and treated in everything and in any way that is not Christian. If we don't follow him, we just won't receive the greater prize that some charismatic leader would persuade us to believe in, but this does not seem like the example that Jesus or the Apostles gave to us, nor any example that Paul gave. When those that wanted to add more than just the blood to salvation condemned Paul, he waited until some believers understood the truth from God and were reconciled back to Paul. If God leads us, we will separate ourselves from those that would use control tactics to keep us in their organization and under their influence. False leaders do this by creating an atmosphere that makes individuals believe they are the only truc follows of Christ. No matter what building you are in or what organization you belong to there is only one church, and no relationship with a dogmatic belief will put you in favor with God.

What happened to the leaders that were servants? When did the charismatic leader take over? Why are we amazed with the individual that can tell us interesting things and keep our minds focused on every word even though they do not show the fruit of the Spirit? These charismatic leaders control whole organizations with a large staff and it is awesome to see their power. They run under the name and doctrines of Christ but do not serve, but rather are served by the saints. This is not the example the Apostles followed or showed to the church. The Apostles did not stay where there was a strong church with no persecution, but led by giving their lives to Christ and setting an example for the church to follow. Their teachings led them to places where they were not wanted and even to their deaths. The Apostles did not live a rich and powerful life but, died for what they believed, as did with many of the first believers.

Even Paul had problems with charismatic leaders that wished to add more to salvation than the forgiveness of sins through the blood of Christ. These so-called Apostles taught that you must also follow Jewish laws and customs in order to be saved. A careful study will show that Paul was not against the following of customs, but wanted the saints to know that conducting rituals and living standards did not save anyone. It may have been good for even the Gentile Christians to follow the customs and laws in order to honor all those that died for God and the

Jewish way of living, but it should be understood that these customs are not what saves you, for only Jesus' blood can save each and every one of us. The addition of living standards and dress codes may show wisdom, but ordinances can never replace a relationship with Christ. Maybe Paul understood that dress codes and living standards evolve into an unholy conduct expressing the evil that resides in every one of us, for this is our human condition.

Unfortunately, as the Gentile church grew, it found other traditions and customs to follow. Many followers took charge and taught that these new ways were the right ways to be Christian and by well formed speech indoctrinated other followers into accepting new belief systems as being important for salvation. It seems as though it is human nature to lean on more than just the blood of Christ. Many leave a relationship with Christ and find comfort in a relationship with some systematic doctrine that is proclaimed to be Christian. When understanding this we can easily see why Jesus said when he returned, will he find faith?

Leaders in the church are supposed to be the servants. Before Gentiles were added into the church, they added a class of leadership that we now know as deacons. Today many words are used, like overseer, pastor, bishop and any name that can define a position in the church. Deacons were created so that the heads of the church could study the word of God and not have to serve in different ways. Even though these men that were picked out were also servants, their position became important in keeping the leadership in a place of servitude. This is what is meant by the first shall be last and the last first. Neither position was put in place in order to control the followers of Christ.

Naming positions in the church is no problem when its purpose is for keeping attitudes of servitude in what is thought of as the leadership. But now we have a mixture of what everyone does in the church; the problem begins when those in authority arc not being servants but exercising power over others and controlling the church. Then we lose the most important part of the structure of what the church is suppose to realize. When leadership takes over instead of serving others, then those that wish to search the Bible to see if the teachings are correct become outcast and the type of study that questions the leadership's interpretation of the Bible is discouraged. We can see that this is not right because Jesus said that it should not be so among his followers; he was referring to the body of Christ, as the disciples would become the foundation for eternity.

> **"It is impossible to find the type of person that is charismatic and also full of the fruit of the Spirit that is not seeking to be in charge of others because this type of saint does not exist."**

Business, government and other worldly organizations seem to follow those that have a strong sense of control and believe they know how to get things done. We call many of these people public or private servants but they are not a type or example of servants that Jesus expected in the church. These men think up great things to say and great plans to execute that seem to expand their worldly organizations. When we accept these types of men as spiritual leaders of Christianity, we do not need the work that God had intended. It is impossible to find the type of person that is charismatic and also full of the fruit of the Spirit and not seeking to be in charge of others because this type of saint does not exist. Churches need to change their concept of leadership to fall in line with the example of what Jesus wanted, or we as members need to find leaders that are full of the Spirit instead of individuals that are wonderful speakers and people that can control others.

THE CHURCH VS. THE WORLD

The church should not mimic the world in its structure and how it does business. Two troubling aspects are political power and idealizing organizations. When a church has political power and when Christians idolize the form of Government that their organization follows, everything changes about what it is to be Christian. Christians that are in political positions would promote their belief system, but the true belief system is in knowing Christ. The more the secular becomes like the sacred, the harder it is to know who is Christian. On the other side of the spectrum, when the people are being put to death for their faith, there is no doubt about which saints really believe. In most societies we have a middle ground between these two situations in relationship to the church's existence.

Only by studying and praying can you know what it is to be Christian. Governmental laws and rules that claim to be Christian or Biblical only exist in the minds of those that do not understand what Christianity is when proclaiming existence. A law that teaches not to kill is no more a Christian virtue than the one that controls the speed on a road. The concepts of seeing a connection between laws and ideas in the Bible are illogical correlations. Those that fight against abortion and fight for prayer in public places do not understand that

Christianity was not meant to control society nor can society control Christianity. Christians should follow laws that are much deeper than what can be put on paper. In fact, the further away the laws are from what is truly Christian, the more the church will realize what it means to be Christian. Churches that are in areas where they are persecuted do not worry about high-minded theology and systematic belief systems but wish only to know Christ.

Another subversive problem is when you believe that your political system is God's system. Anyone that truly knows and walks with God realizes that there is no government system on this earth that represents God. Even today many proudly proclaim they are in a non-denominational church with the idea that they believe that being interdenominational is the correct type of Church structure that God wants the saints to belong to and participate in while the church is on the earth. Non-denominational is a form of Government structure, but many are led to believe that it means inter-denominational. Non-denominational has nothing or little to do with the dogmatic beliefs of the organization. In other words, if Christians mean interdenominational, they don't exclude anyone from being Christian, for this statement claims that they are not judgmental. This notion comes from our belief in tolerance derived from our Governmental philosophical foundation. Of course, people in denominational churches can also not be judgmental as the word denominational only refers to its governmental structure. This situation exists as church members are not taught critical thinking, but only learn the religious language from their local members. The confusion of words is another problem, just as when the words *public* or *private servant* are used, but don't point to a position of servitude.

This is the same problem when referring to a position of authority as a servitude position. We can see that in the beginning history of the Church there were many problems mostly because of the Gentiles entering the community. Some believed that the Gentiles should follow the Jewish laws that so many had died for and others believed the Gentiles did not have to follow these rules. Well, maybe both positions were correct. You don't have to follow the Jewish customs to be saved, but it is very honorable to follow these customs and show homage to those that have died.

FALSE FRUITS

Christians can display a false humility that is really a "puffed up" humbleness. False leaders believe because they are so "humble" they are the greatest among the saints. These leaders hide behind what is thought to be a true Christian virtue in order to control those in the church that will consider them as important. True humility can be seen when Paul was fighting with those that would add rules to salvation. He wrote about all the marks on his body and the times he was in prison, but he proclaimed himself as the least of all the saints for he once persecuted the followers of Jesus. Humbleness is something you have, not something you practice, and if you are only practicing it, your true virtues will show later when you are unaware. That is why you can copy the fruit of the Spirit, but for only so long. When God changes you, it is a complete change where the fruit manifests itself as part of your being.

Christians will always have a war within themselves as the fleshly desires fight against the Spirit's. If this fight ceases to exist in your life, then you should examine yourself to see if you really have a relationship with God. False teachers and false saints will not have this war within them. Although we cannot see within someone's subjective thoughts and feelings, we can become sensitive to the Spirit and find hidden sin that is within us by seeing sin in others. In other words, when we notice some personal sin within someone else, it is because that sin resides within us and we project it on to another person, as this is a human condition. If we are full of love from the Spirit, we become blind to others sins, as when a natural love is present between people, they will be blind to each partner's shortcomings.

FIRST LEADERS DIE

The first to die for being a Christian was a leader. This deacon was considered the first martyr. Soon additional leaders followed; God spared some leaders only to allow their deaths later. As we can see, this leader was chosen to wait on the tables of those that needed help, for he was filled with the fruit of the Spirit. He was not picked because he could give a good sermon, or because he looked nice, or even because he could say interesting things, but because of his Spirit-filled attitude. As the church grew in number it took on many of what we today would call ministries and waiting on tables may have been the first. Waiting on tables and taking care of certain types of people in different situations is the leadership position that was given to Stephen. He was a leader by example, but many today do not follow such practices. The church needs more people that are willing to serve and less people that want to claim a position of prophet or evangelist or any other position that elevates them before the assemble.

Even these positions are meant to serve the body in order for it to grow correctly.

Those that serve in such a capacity will not be well known in the church, or even in the world, but will receive a reward in heaven. The religious leaders received their reward while serving in the temple from people's awe and respect. But if you are a servant, no one will realize that you are serving unless they need something and then the recognition, if any, will be short. It is hard to tell if we are going to receive our reward after death or before, but within all of us we already know unless we wish to be blind. The test is: are you noticed and are you elevated for the work that you do while being in service to the saints or being controlled by the fruit of the Spirit that is in you.

DEATH BED CONFESSIONS

This story is not addressing deathbed confessions. But it may refer to how much you get for how much work you have done in the body of Christ. If that is applied to salvation, then we will all receive the same reward. One coin is all that each received as they served in the vineyard. The most important reward is eternal life. That is all the saint should care about when considering what work to do. The concept of servitude has been changed in the church. When someone is picked for a leadership position, it is considered a place of authority. Servitude is not authority and no matter what type of name you give a position of authority and claim it is for serving, it will in fact never be service. We can all get wrapped up in deep theology on what eternity is like, but it is said that we cannot even imagine what the afterlife is like. Maybe that is why the Bible is so vague when talking about what it will be like in the new place. This is why we should rejoice because we are saved and not for any other reason. There are many books written on the subject of what the afterlife is like and who will be there, but the Bible only gives a glimpse of it and really cannot explain it because it is beyond our finite comprehension.

The deathbed confession will always be disputed, but the truth is that we have no way to judge. God at the end knows what is and isn't true. Even when we live and walk with God, it is hard to know whether someone really is a child of God or not. For even Satan is seen as an angel of light. It is easy to be mistaken about who to follow and who not to follow. The one on the cross asked Jesus for forgiveness, but we cannot be sure that this is an exception or the norm. The one thing that we can be sure is that it is a judgment call that will always be examined over and over again, asked by every generation. The more that one believes in a merciful God, the more one will accept any doctrine of deathbed confessions.

ANTIRELIGIOUS

There are two anti-religious themes seen in this parable. One is what the parable is about and that is to be a leader you must be a servant, not a servant in name but one in action. That is why the first was last and last was first. There are many religions in the world and within those religions there are many trains of thought. Many of these people are to be followed and also worshiped. You must discipline yourself to become like them. Their disciples wait on them and they grow rich and famous, as is true in some of the organizations in the church, but the truth is that none of the Apostles grew rich from preaching while in the world. In fact, they gave up everything to follow Jesus. You cannot change yourself, but can only let the Spirit change you and help you grow in the fruit of the Spirit.

The second anti-religious theme is the murmuring to the vineyard owner and that is a type of complaining to God as the vineyard owner represents God. These were people that were not satisfied with what God gave them. They are the ones that believe they deserve more. We have these kinds of people in the church and the world. They proclaim their greatness but God humbles them with wisdom. Or sometimes what they have in this world is all they will ever have, for they will receive nothing in the afterlife. This is why you see so many people get much more in life than they deserve, because God's love gives them something while they are still alive on earth knowing that they will never accept eternal life.

Even the phrase "kingdom of God" is an anti-religious statement and was a thorn in the flesh to the Jewish community. They were under the power of Rome and had to compromise their situation because Rome claimed to be the only kingdom and power. Jesus' proclamation was a direct attack against Rome itself, but Jesus was not attacking Rome per se but the concept of the power behind Rome. Jesus was not a political movement at that time, for he even said that is kingdom was not of this world which is why his followers don't fight.

The ethical phenomenon from the parable suggests that you should be happy for what others receive and not grumble and complain. This complaining, seen in business, government and even in the church, does not come from the Spirit and is an attack on the self, as the self wants to be exulted. Why we would complain about our position in the church seems somewhat naïve, except for the fact that it isn't the servants that are running the churches today; unfortunately, this fact is easily seen by outsiders. Why we would complain about someone getting promoted in the world, or in the church, is because of our self-centered sin, as our subjective self governed by the flesh does not wish to walk in the Spirit. So if you want to be the greatest in the kingdom of God, you must be the servant. You must wait on the saints, but just because you take a position without pay does not mean you are in a servitude position. Nor will you be great in the kingdom if you work in order to be exulted in respect to the eternal when in truth you want to look pious and respected by others is sin. Godly leadership by servitude comes only through the fruit of the Spirit. It is this fruit that will draw the outsider to Christ and not some exulted position.

FEMINISM

The Bible probably is the most feminist book written, although there are leaders in the church who do not take on a true servant's role who like to use parts of the Christian text to put women in a role of servitude to men. We should understand that all that are in Christ are equal and that you should esteem others as greater than yourself. But this concept of women-servitude interpretation is so far removed from what the writers were trying to explain in the Christian text that it is a wonder that this doctrine is not questioned more. This attitude of not questioning the interpretations of belittling women just shows that something has changed for the worse in the Church.

The Bible gives many examples of leaders that were women. It was foretold that women would have dreams and visions. But in order to promote sexual inequality, all of these parts of the Bible must be put on the back burner or hidden with some perverse talk in order to keep them unknown to those that do not study and question. A man is to give up his life for his woman while the woman is told to honor her man. Because of the differences between men and women, this explanation on how each should treat the other makes both equal. The verses that say that the woman is not to speak in the meeting is actually a reference to fact the husband and wife are to discuss controversial situations at home and then come to church with the same opinion, not that women are not allowed to speak while in a church environment. It is not as we may have been told that the woman is to give her opinion at home and if the man, being the head and leader, decides differently, then that is it, for his opinion rules. No, they both must come to an agreement through prayer and study or both should keep silent until they are of one opinion on any subject.

There are some women named in the Christian text as being deacons, but those that want to control people's thoughts and have the power over saints do not mention such passages by Paul. It is astonishing to see how many people believe they know the Bible yet miss the simplest things and can only quote those ideas that come from their dogmatic views. When you only know the passages that elevate your dogmatic views, then you have not studied, but have just accepted someone's point of view. This is a problem with us and causes division that we accept because we are not walking in the Spirit like we should.

CHAPTER 7
THE RICH MAN

The unexamined life is not worth living.
Socrates (The Last Days of Socrates)

Examine yourselves to see whether you are in the faith; test yourselves. Do you not realize that Christ Jesus is in you—unless, of course, you fail the test?

2 Corinthians: 13:5 (The Bible—New International Version)

A ROSE BY ANY OTHER NAME IS NOT A ROSE

This story is not about paradoxes; it is a good story to explore and understand the concept that all dogma and existence comes to a paradoxical conclusion. The Christian writings are the tradition of the Church and were preserved for us that would be born much later. It is best to try to find out what was really meant by the stories and concepts preserved for learning and not to use verses and stories to promote our way of living or dogmatic views. We need to sort out the meaning of scriptures through prayer, fasting and studying. Its amazes me that Christians do not want to learn the original languages of the Bible along with a historical understanding of how people thought in Biblical times. We become complacent with what the church teaches and accept what is taught.

Although many of us do not have the time to study all aspects of the Bible, shame comes when those that do have the time have no desire, or want to reinforce what they believe without examining it for possible errors. We all have fallen into this complacency many times with many concepts, instead of doubting what we have been taught and searching to find the truth about ourselves and the meaning of Biblical knowledge.

Do we understand the stories that Jesus told as he meant us to understand them? Or do we apply modern day understandings in order to justify our dogmatic beliefs? The disciples and others that listened to Jesus had a hard time accepting and understanding what he said because the Biblical teachings of Jesus' day were something very different than what Jesus was proclaiming. It is possible that those that taught in Jesus' day tainted the common person, just as our understanding of parts of the Bible are misunderstood because of what we were taught. If you heard the correct teaching, would you reject it because those that are in authority do not believe that it is right? Let us assume that Jesus used the name of Lazarus in order to existentially incorporate Lazarus' resurrection into this parable. What then if this parable's title was changed to What the Raising of Mary and Martha's brother taught us to understand? The outcome would be a parable that has been misunderstood by most Biblically religious-minded people. The changing of the title can change the way you look at the parable. It is difficult to remove yourself from the knowledgebase which you inherited at birth, because this knowledgebase has its preconceptions.

Can we remove ourselves from our environment and really see what Jesus may have been trying to teach? The experiences that we have within our environment strongly influence our choices and understandings through life. How much do we understand because of our social upbringing? We need to step out of the confinement of our preconceptions to really understand what was going on in those days in relationship to what Jesus was doing and saying. With this knowledge, if it can be obtained, we can investigate understandings that are the norm for the reader and the writer of the works when first set to paper. For this reason, because it is almost impossible and some would argue is impossible, many are led by misdirection. We tend to view this story as a teaching of the condemnation of wealth; someone of wealth being condemned for having a good life and someone that had not much of a life given a place next to Abraham in paradise. Does this parable condemn the rich man because he was rich or because of his unbelief, like that of his brothers?

It is easy to see that you can answer these questions with yes/no and explain systematically the reason why your interpretation is correct. Many people may believe that an understanding is right, or that none are right, in relationship to other parts of the Bible. If the Spirit of God can only give you a correct understanding of the Bible, then those that do not have his Spirit cannot really know which if any explanations are right. Those led by the Spirit can critically examine text, but this cannot be done if Christians have not been taught critical thinking. To those without the Spirit, the Bible is just a book to read just like any other book. It cannot be applied if they do not have God drawing them to understand His word. Enforcement of belief in the inerrant or infallible Word of God may be vain as theologians and Bible teachers need to understand that if someone has the Spirit, apologetics are not needed because we know the truth through Jesus Christ. But since the Spirit must lead us individually into all truth, we need educational tools for the Spirit to move us from faith to faith.

A problem defining riches could be the beginning of one of the beliefs that a very anti-materialistic understanding is holy, and the claim that being spiritual is the same as being anti-materialistic. This is a concept found in many of the first heresies at the beginning of Christianity, which many scholars believed evolved into Christian Gnosticism. The first known heresies to enter Christianity had anti-materialistic tendencies that have influenced Christian teachings even until this day, although the belief systems that carried anti-materialistic concepts to the extreme were condemned by orthodoxy. Dioecism, known as the first wrong understanding to enter Christianity, could not accept that God came in the flesh; therefore this belief had anti-materialistic tendencies. This belief was centered on the first disagreements in understanding who Jesus the Christ was and still is in argument promoted by many today. These followers could not accept that the immaterial God could put on substance. The arguments against these heretical teachings developed into what we know as the doctrine of the Trinity.

LAZARUS' NAME

The Hebrews of Jesus time understood this story in context. There would have been no misunderstanding about what this story was talking about. The rich man represented not just someone who had wealth and position, but is an indication of someone that is also rich in religious knowledge: a Pharisee. When this rich man spoke to Abraham about his brothers, the reply was that they already had Moses and the prophets and revealed that the brothers did not really believe Moses and the prophets or the brothers would not have been heading, in their death, to the same place as the dead rich man. He also called Abraham father, a basic belief of the Pharisees on how they obtained salvation. But when the dead man asked to send the poor man on a mission to tell the brothers of their destiny, Abraham said they would not believe even if someone rose from the dead. This had a double meaning; that Jesus himself would rise from the dead and that Lazarus had or was to be raised from the dead.

The differences in the raisings are that Jesus raised both himself and Lazarus, as Lazarus was unable to raise himself from death. Yet, the Pharisees would not believe in Jesus even after he raised Lazarus from the dead, another indication that the Pharisees didn't even believe their own religions views. For the Pharisees, according to their dogma, if one could raise someone from the dead then that one could also forgive sin. In other words, raising someone from the dead or healing someone was no different than forgiving sin. Sin caused both death and bad health either to the one who sinned or to someone in the family of the one who had sinned.

But the use of Lazarus' name also would remind those that heard him, as well as the Pharisees, that Jesus had brought another man, also named Lazarus, back from the dead. Or, if the story had been told before the death of Lazarus, then the event would remind people of the parable. Whether Lazarus was raised from the dead came before or after this story is not significant. But this is probably why the name Lazarus was used in this parable.

Also, these writings were not made until after the beginning of the church.

Well, what do you believe about the coincidence of Jesus using the name of Lazarus and also raising someone named Lazarus from the dead? This example would be interpreting the Bible from the Bible, not through insight that could be called revelation or enlightenment, or through support from religious dogmatic teachings.

The story of the rich man and Lazarus is about faith and the content of the lecture Jesus gives after it is about faith and the paradox of faith, because knowledge puts one in a paradoxical situation. We must accept one point of knowledge or its paradoxical view.

TRADITION CLOUDS
THE TRUTH OF THE GOSPEL

Modern day interpretation of the Bible is not completely wrong in what it proclaims, but history and tradition can cloud the real understanding of what was meant to be taught by the stories. We should bear that in mind when interpreting any portion of the Biblical text. Didn't the Pharisees have much of their understanding correct? Yes, many Pharisees did accept the teachings of Jesus before and after the birth of the church. The Pharisees' acceptance of Christ is recorded only latently so as not to damage the hidden antireligious tone of the Christian writings. The religious leader's teachings also blinded people to what was really important in respect to the philosophy of the Bible. If the teachers had not been so blind, they would have taught the common people in such a way that most all would have accepted John the Baptist and Jesus.

Furthermore, you can latently see that the Biblical scholars knew that what Jesus was teaching was correct, even though they did not tell the public for fear that they would lose what they had gained in regard to their social wealth and position. This is probably the reason why they attacked both John the Baptist's and Jesus' character. They could not use their dogmatic interpretations, because Jesus would show how it contradicted the Bible. The Biblical scholars tried to use scripture, but were wrong because they didn't know the true birthplace of Jesus and facts. Of course those that believed in Christ wrote the historical information.

As Paul said, we see dimly, not completely. Paraphrasing even points out that Paul did not believe that he knew the complete truth, and that we would only know when we are changed, when we see Jesus appear. But this parable, when seen as a symbolic one that shows Jesus' attempt to teach the Pharisees that they didn't have their religious views correct, is more in line with Jesus' interactions with the Pharisees. For the Pharisees believed their teachings were correct, just as some churches today may believe, or we even may personally believe, that we have the right understanding, the right dogmatic views, and the right interpretations of the Bible.

That is if we are ethnocentric with what is important and what we believe we know about the Bible. But Christianity is no more ethnocentric than Judaism is racist or the Christian writings are anti-Jewish. All the racist ideals in the Bible are really antireligious. Hebrews were not to marry with other nations, because of heathen worship. Christians are not to marry anyone that isn't a Christian. Is this because both are antireligious? Maybe when we understand the whole of what God is, then we will know the truth. So what are the Pharisees and our condition?

PARABLES ARE ANTIRELIGIOUS
AND PARADOXICAL

Because Jesus was addressing the condition of the Pharisees, the story becomes one of many parables that can be interpreted as latently anti-religious. It is like all of Jesus' parables that may be understood as symbolic and anti-religious even though some modern interpretations may have reasons to understand it as a worldview and one way to formulating dogma or a paradigm of knowledge. Unfortunately, we can become very dogmatic about a position that is not meant to be of any importance to Christianity, or apply it outwardly instead of existentially. For Jesus often spoke of what was in us and not what we could just see in the world.

The Paradoxes through this story are very important because existence is a paradox. We can understand that there are paradoxes in life when we read this parable and ask questions like: Is it ok to be rich? Do all poor go to heaven? Why did Jesus condemn those that believed in and tried to follow the Bible in a religious manner? Paradoxes create questions and many paradoxes may not have answers. But without paradoxes we would all see the world the same way, and there would be no debate on what is right or wrong. When Adam and Even partook of the tree of knowledge of good and evil, they did not receive perfect knowledge of good and evil, just an existential knowledge. In fact, this knowledge was existential and can be seen in the way Adam and Eve reacted to this new insight.

Jesus did not teach that existence is a paradox, but one can understand why faith is so important when knowledge is confronted with paradoxes. Jesus uses this paradox of knowledge to confront the religious-minded people. Specifically, Jesus uses this paradox that is inherent in all knowledge to confront the Pharisees.

PARABLES ARE NOT WORLD VIEWS

In church, you may have learned about heaven and hell through this story. If you did, were you convinced that the lesson taught was correct? Or are we misunderstanding Jesus' intent when we view this story as a truth that there is a paradise and hell? This story is probably not an indication of the existence of paradise and hell or of the negation of the same, but it should be understood that just because we are religious doesn't mean that a religious life and knowledge will get us to heaven. In fact, many of the religious people of Jesus' time were basing their beliefs on the Bible. These people were Bible believers. This is one paradox: that we must be religious to be saved, but religion doesn't save. So religion for some saves, as for others it condemns. It's odd that studying the Bible cannot only lead to the truth, but can also send us into believing we are saved even though we are far from being a child of God. The ambiguity of existence sets in on all of our being. We see that everything is not black or white; even the different shades between are hard to explain or understand. And so we struggle with trying to find out what is right and pleases God. Many today claim that they know, but do we?

Dogmatic views such as "once saved, always saved" can be exercised within a systematic theology, but shows the limits of human understanding when considering the parable Jesus taught that the tare and wheat grow together. So how can we tell the difference between wheat and tare when someone proclaims to be a Christian? How would anyone claim to know for sure? If you take this dogmatic belief to its ultimate conclusion, you can only see that it is meaningless. This meaninglessness is the human condition. But on the other hand, the other view is also meaningless in the fact that just because we say we believe isn't proof of what we are, since we cannot see within others and also can deceive ourselves.

Not only is it meaningless, but in most Christian individuals it creates an atmosphere of pride. One can only proudly proclaim eternal salvation whether predestined or free choice. Whether one is correct in knowing about salvation is probably only known by God. Paul knew that his time was at hand and he had fought a good fight, because he received the knowledge from God through his relationship and not by blind faith or the acceptance of a dogmatic position.

Christians that are not sure of eternal salvation can also become proud of their humility. So we can become proud with the opinions we have no matter what position we choose. What do you believe about salvation? Are you proud that you have the correct understanding? Only subjectively can you see yourself and examine whether you condemn others as you devalue those that do not accept your viewpoint. The only way to truly see yourself is by examining yourself through the Bible, a mirror in which you can clearly see yourself; if you walk away forgetting what you have seen or not applying what you have learned, then you know what you have done.

When we look at a belief in more detail, considering free will, acceptance neglects the awesome power of God, for that is what the term *God* implies. To say that we have free will is to say that God is not in control. Many theologians have spent their lives analyzing this paradox without resolution, yet today there are two schools of thought that will not accept each other, refusing to understand their

THE ANTIRELIGIOUS VIEWS OF JESUS AS EXPRESSED IN HIS PARABLES

own weaknesses and contradictions. Anything less than a God omnipotent and omniscient does not fit the definition of what the term God implies. What is the definition of God? Is God powerful enough to give free will? Or should God? There are verses written that God's will does not always happen and that God cannot lie. Yet every Christian wants to believe that God is controlling lives and can do all things.

GOD IS EXISTENCE, NOT ESSENCE

The Christian writings speak very little of the essence of God, but do speak about God's existence. When the Bible speaks on the essence of God, it uses symbolic language, because words cannot really express the true essence of the Creator. Some things about the essence of God are inferred. Being is not the argument about God's existence, but when referring to God the Bible points towards how you can know God existentially. Of course, God does not exist as a being, but God is being. God is not another thing like you and I or like a tree or flower. You are a being, but God is being. God can never be the object but only the subject. The correct way to talk about God is with subjective thought. Referring to God as object is misguided and anthropomorphic, and produces error as we try to understand God.

Another analogy makes this story symbolic of the Gospel: Lazarus is a type of Christ being raised from the dead, as well as a true believer, Moses and the prophets are the witnesses of the resurrection to come, and the Pharisees are a type of false believers. Here we can see the death, burial and resurrection of Jesus and thirst after righteousness and believe is what is witnessed in the true believers. The rich man had colors of royalty and religious

Biblical concepts attached to him since while in torment he spoke of Abraham as father. And the crumbs of his life were given to Lazarus that hungered so much for bread; he died to himself and life even as the dogs were licking at his sores. These dogs could be symbolic of humanity and how it treats the poor in life. Not poor as in owning worldly goods, but poor as in being, or poor as in religious manner would fit if we consider those that are not good enough for us to befriend in our everyday life.

The paradox that Lazarus and others were raised from the dead is not an issue when one is concerned with what was so important about Jesus' resurrection. This paradox is avoided by not claiming Lazarus' raising was a resurrection or a pre-resurrection. Lazarus coming back to life was a much different resurrection than what we shall experience in the last day. There still is a profound paradox in the different resurrections as Jesus was the only one that could self-raise. Lazarus did not change in any manner except for his new experience, but everyday life will change us as we go through any experience, or even the negation of any experience.

TRUE PARADOX AND ETHNOCENTRISM

The most important true paradox is Jesus being fully man and fully God at the same time. All other paradoxes are created from some type of rational knowledge and are subordinate to this paradox. You cannot take two things such as lemons and water, mix them together, and expect lemonade to be completely water and completely lemons at the same time. There must be a percentage of each of them. Jesus being completely God and completely man is not just some religious language but is something that God can do that man cannot. The godhead confusion is grounded in this rational and irrational acceptance and divides the mature and immature Christian, as well as those that can and cannot believe.

Christianity teaches that Jesus is the only way. Does this mean that Christians arc narrow minded or ethnocentric? No, not when you understand what Jesus being the only way means. This is mentioned in the Gospel of John and is addressed to those that believe some knowledge would bring them to salvation. John is teaching the Gnostic believer that only Jesus is the way and they need no more knowledge. In a non-Gnostic sense it would imply that once you know Jesus, you can follow no better way. This implies that all are in the place of the Gnostic when they do not have a relationship with Christ. Therefore, no matter what belief system you follow, in some respect a religion leads to the following of Christ or the religion leads you away from the true God of the universe. This ethnocentric view is encapsulated in the two world views.

There are other short parables, sayings, really; these also explain the meaning that Jesus is the only way. Many sayings teach us that when we find Jesus, we cannot understand any better way. We will give everything we have, even our lives, to follow Jesus. So, if God has made other ways for everlasting life, the Christian paradigm is blind to this, for we only can say as Paul said in Romans— all are judged by their own master. We cannot judge them, but can only show why we believe in Christ. Just like Christianity, all religious beliefs have some latent ethnocentric view. Even the non-religious have some latent ethnocentric view, which is evidence that ethnocentrism is not a religious manifestation but a human condition.

Furthermore, we can become so dogmatic in personal beliefs that we cannot see the paradox of our beliefs. The

Pharisees were so dogmatic that they couldn't deny their teaching even after Jesus pointed out the contradictions. Many of their teachings pointed to Jesus as being the Messiah, but other teachings perverted the Bible. How much more can our Christian views resurrect the attitude of religious leaders, that the Pharisees were merely a type of, but have existed in all civilizations throughout history? Even Cain wanted God to accept his religion his way. Cain seems to show the same self-centered traits that all individuals do when confronted with the paradox of their knowledge.

Jesus was directing this story at the Pharisees, implying that the rich man was a type of Pharisee. The paradox is easily seen, in that those whom the rich man was trying to save from his own fate were religious because they knew of Moses and the prophets. Jesus was implying that although the Pharisees knew the teachings of Moses and the prophets, they didn't really believe. The Pharisees understood this story and that is why they continued mocking. They knew it was directed toward them, but they were so grounded in their own systematic philosophy that they could not see their own errors and continued to justify all the paradoxes within their paradigm. The author also latently teaches us that since the Pharisees understood the parable—while the listeners may not have comprehended, the Pharisees were without excuse.

Theology is strictly Christian and there used to be an obvious parallel between the beliefs of Biblical times and modern religious beliefs. Paul was the first theologian, as he is an example of those that should be called theologians. A theologian is one that believes in the death, burial and resurrection of Christ. Like Paul, we must always examine our belief and ourselves. This is what pushed Paul to go to Jerusalem and talk to the Apostles.

We are not to be like the Pharisees that were taught the dogmatic views and accepted them without questioning. Many today are like the Pharisees and cannot examine their belief systems and see the Biblical contradictions, in the paradigms, of their knowledge.

PHARISEES HAD NO REAL LOVE

The parable leaves out any love between the rich man and Lazarus. An example of a paradigm is the Pharisees legalism and their expression of caring for others. They took pride in their compassionate assistance and maybe understood this need from the content of the Bible. So the Bible, when understood in its correct context, teaches that we should have the same moral beliefs that would drive us to care about those that are in need. But, the Pharisees didn't help the poor to the extent that their own life would suffer. Paul wrote about this and explained that if we didn't do it with love, it had no meaning. This is understood because the Paradox that God became a man was created out of love, the very thing that God is, and that defines his deity existentially.

That God came down to earth and died on the cross in the person of Jesus is the focal point of the Bible. If the Pharisees had really believed in Moses and the prophets, they would have had the same love as Christ. But this love is existential and is a paradox in that without love you can still commit acts of love. The paradox of love is shown in its completeness when contemplating Christ in God.

Jesus being fully God and fully man at the same time is this fulfillment of love. This paradox is understood in that when you combine two things, the outcome cannot be a complete whole of each thing. You have either a new thing or a portion of each to make the whole. Water and lemons make lemonade, but it is not totally lemon and totally water as stated before. But Jesus was totally God and totally man at the same time. Without this paradox as our paradigm, no other paradoxes can be correctly understood existentially. All concepts become demonic when we leave out Christ, for if Christ is correct, then all religion, science and philosophy that is not based on him must be tainted in some respect, except for the hard sciences that need no hypothesis.

The belief that one will prosper when becoming a Christian and that the rich are somewhat destined for hell because of their riches is a paradox within itself. A misunderstanding arises when one sees this story as a condemnation of those that are rich, as Abraham himself is believed to have been rich. So this story is better understood as an indictment against those that are rich in religious knowledge and not in wealth, or Abraham would be in torment with the rich man in hell. Furthermore, those that trust in riches are contrary to Abraham's faith. He, like Job, was rich in faith and possessions. The Pharisees believed that their riches were a blessing from God, as many still believe in their hearts and teach today. Whether they express it verbally or dogmatically, they manifest it personally in the way they live.

Are riches good or bad? Do riches send one to hell? If this story is talking about rich in religious matters, then why did the religious man end up in hell? These are all questions showing that existence is a paradox. The only way you overcome this paradox is by faith. Without faith, answers bring more paradoxical questions. With knowledge you can ignore the paradox of any concept, but the paradox still exist. All dogmatic statements contain paradoxes, and that is why you can accept it or its opposite view. Even when you bring paradoxes into harmony with each other through philosophy or theology, the paradox remains and cannot be resolved. Without paradoxes philosophers, theologians and many writings would have nothing to discuss or resolve. So as to the question of riches and eternity, the answer cannot be contained in one sentence. How important is wealth and religious understanding? The Pharisees may have mocked Jesus, because they saw the story as an indictment between their rich and poor and could not see the true meaning, but this seems somewhat absurd. If they had not understood the parable, they would have wondered about the meaning and not mocked Jesus.

The rich man represented those that were wealthy in religious knowledge and lived in a high religious state, as the poor man represented those that understood their human condition and sinful nature. The poor are happy to partake of the leftover food that was not eaten by the rich man; these crumbs represented God's grace that the rich man, if taken as a representation of a Pharisee, did not teach. This is easily understood when we realize that faith is existential and rises above the paradox of knowledge.

Abraham represented teachings that are from God, as the rich man represents the religious Pharisees' teachings that are contrary to faith. The Pharisee's religion was based on knowledge that is systematic and makes sense when interpreting the Bible, but this systematic knowledge hides its own paradoxes, as well as the faith that is existential.

Furthermore, the Pharisees religion was based on the Bible, but their life did not follow the same subjective faith that Abraham had in regards to what wealth meant. Abraham's wealth had nothing to do with subjective faith and a religious life, but the Pharisees taught that their physical wealth came from God. They taught that because of their religious life they were Abraham's children. The Pharisees probably justified their wealth by teaching that

God blessed Abraham with wealth. Abraham became wealthy in spite of the many mistakes in his life in relation to his subjective faith. Abraham's wealth came by the promise in that he believed in God, not because of his faith.

CHRISTIAN PARADOX

The problem of wealth is paradoxical within Christianity. Knowledge, life style and wealth are something that can be understood subjectively differently. The problem is that we cannot see the other's subjective ideas, so we cannot judge someone by their wealth, religious life, or by what they believe. Although the Christian text speaks against such judgmental attitudes, that Christians continually think this way shows that they do not regard the Bible with much respect. Knowledge has not yet come into non-existence so the paradoxes still remain. Having the Spirit and following the Spirit seems to be two different attitudes. It seems that the attitude of unjust judgments will continue in the church despite the Christian text's condemnation of such acts.

Many theologians claim that this was not just a parable but also a true story because a personal pronoun was used. There may be some truth to this, but even if this is a different kind of parable, the question that should be asked is not if these where real individuals, or that this is a world view that all Christians should have, but, "what was Jesus trying to teach?" Why would Jesus mention a man by name? Does the name Lazarus mean something? Even if this explanation is the correct one, it doesn't change the meaning of the story, nor is it easy to prove; it can only be accepted on faith based on knowledge and not

THE ANTIRELIGIOUS VIEWS OF JESUS AS EXPRESSED IN HIS PARABLES

subjective faith that exists above the paradox of understanding.

Another problem with understanding this parable as being a story about real people is that there is no other part of the Bible that confirms this teaching. If the Bible is to be used to interpret the Bible, then we with this view should find other parts of the Bible to back up this concept, or we will have to accept the belief that human authority interprets the Bible and not the Bible itself. If the position of human authority is correct, then one should probably accept Apostolic Succession. Therefore, to accept the traditional teaching that this explains where you go when you die is somewhat absurd. Furthermore, other verses contradict this version of paradise and hell separated by a gulf. Also, the idea that this is a real story adds nothing to what Jesus was trying to teach the audience.

These arguments seem to stem from the teachings that the Bible has no errors or is infallible or both. Yet if the word of God is Spiritual and can only be understood by those that have the Spirit, then to those that do not have God's Spirit it is just a book of history, literature, morals and philosophy. So if you try to prove that the Bible is perfect in some aspect to those without the Spirit, wouldn't you think that is like eating the cow before you kill and prepare it? This is probably why Paul never got into trying to change secular laws as some do today. Paul was concerned with the individual knowing Christ. A metaphysical understanding of reality was not the topic during this time, but the subject was the Pharisees. The blatant disregard for interpreting this parable as a reprimand against the Pharisee's attitude was probably spawned by someone with Pharisaic tendencies. Many of the arguments in commentaries seem misplaced as these contentions did not exist during the time of the writings.

Jesus was confronting the Pharisees about their dogmatic beliefs during the discussion that was taking place with those that he was teaching. The Pharisees believed they were rich and saved because they were Abraham's children, and that God had blessed them not only with religious knowledge, but also with a good life. In the proceeding parable Jesus attacks their love of money and their religious belief. The Pharisees were known for giving to the poor and helping the less fortunate, but wouldn't do it to a point that they would lose their status in society. Because of their belief system, if a Pharisee lost his status, the change would be the same as sin and condemnation from God.

The story of the unjust servant was a condemnation of their religious attitudes when it comes to understanding what the Pharisees believed. The Pharisees judged everyone harshly concerning the law, as the Pharisees forgot to teach and practice that part of the law that contained mercy. In the end, the unjust servant ignorantly practiced what the lawgiver was trying to express, which he had not done before. That is perhaps why he may have been up for dismissal. If one were to take this story at face value it would be easy to deduct that Jesus was saying it was all right to steal as long as one prospered. Of course this is not the teaching that comes out of this parable. The teaching is that we should share our good fortune with others, for sharing in this fashion is a wise idea just as God shares his creation with us. Or maybe this has been an example of what the Pharisees needed to change in their lives? Was the act of changing what was owed an analogy of forgiveness? Yes, and much more, for it revealed the true intent of the Mosaic Law. In conclusion, the rich man in this story was glad that the manager actually lost him much wealth, even though he was going to fire him for somewhat the same offense. This shows the paradox of knowledge. How can God bless us with wealth and yet ask that same wealth be given away freely? To understand this story is to understand the paradox of knowledge.

As you can easily see, when Jesus was confronting the Pharisees with the story of the *Rich man and Lazarus*, he was continuing his thoughts about both religious and worldly wealth. The paradox within this setting is a perplexing one until we realize that we cannot stand on our own rationalization, but must derive our knowledge from faith in Christ. Furthermore, faith should be a trust in Christ's faith, not our own faith that is easily puffed up in pride and presumption.

It would be absurd to think of this story as setting our understanding of the existence of a heaven and hell. Why would Jesus take time to tell them a story to teach them a concept about a heaven and hell? Jesus would not, but he would use the concepts to let them know they were not destined for heaven just because God had blessed them with both religious knowledge and wealth. In fact, the story never mentions heaven or hell, and this interpretation is a 'leap of faith' as taught by religious people today, not the leap that Kierkegaard taught; so this modern evolutionary day teaching can only come from a pre-doctrinal worldview.

Through these parables and others you can latently see that all systematic theology ends up with a problem of contradictions. No intellectual person can ever go beyond these paradoxes and overcome them, even if others follow the teachings as being true. The only way that you can rise above these paradoxes is to understand the Bible as teaching faith that is existential, with Jesus as the center. Every parable tried to do just this, in that while looking at what Jesus was teaching the Pharisees concerning their religious knowledge, you can look at your own religious knowledge in the same manner. When you rely on the faith of your systematic dogma, you cannot live by faith in Christ. We can either have a relationship with Christ through faith in Him, or have a relationship with Dogma through faith in it. Every Christian must choose faith in dogma or faith in Christ. When we believe that both objects of faith are the same, we become adulterous and demonic.

While in torment, the rich man tries to correct God's theology by explaining that the religious people, his brothers, will believe if someone was raised from the dead. As we know today, this is not true. There is also nothing that proves that the story is about the Gentiles being accepted and the Jewish nation being rejected by God. Nowhere in the Christian text does it mention this parable and say that its interpretation is about the rich man representing the Jewish nation and Lazarus representing the Gentiles. If such were the case, Jesus would have probably used a Gentile name instead of Lazarus. This type of interpretation leads to racism and contradictions concerning love. The tradition that hell and paradise are next to each other with a great gulf between and that this is where people go after they die must be forced into the Christian texts and is not found anywhere else in the Bible.

CHAPTER 8
SAYINGS: SHORT PARABLES

Youth is easily deceived because it is quick to hope.
Aristotle (Rhetoric)

And now these three remain: faith, hope and love. But the greatest of these is love.

1 Corinthians 13:13 (The Bible—New International Version)

GOSPEL OF LOVE

Whenever sound doctrine is mentioned, the section always contains a comment regarding love, as the doctrine of faith and sound belief is embedded in love. Christian texts give a couple of examples of false workers. Paul implies that they confirm a belief system that they do not really understand, for that is because systematic concepts are human made and express doctrine. Only by the Spirit can you know the truth and not by some creed written on paper many years ago. Paul also wrote against the love of money and mentions to Timothy to follow what is important; one of the concepts he was admonished to follow was love. Yet in churches today, you hear more about money than you do love. Paul also writes to everyone about those that forsook him, but prayed that they would not be judged accordingly, as God will judge those that fought against the faith. This shows the love that embraced Paul, as love was something that he was and not what he did.

Paul tells Titus that those that teach false things can be known by their actions; as they deny the existence of God even though they speak about Jesus. They are pushy with their beliefs, alienating anyone that contradicts them. But as long as Titus is being a good example through the fruit of love that was given him, he can show false brethren the truth and maybe they will change. He also informs Titus to have the ones strong in faith teach the weak in faith, and to act respectfully, as this is the spirit of love. Weak in faith refers to those that are new converts, not those that seem to have little faith. This type of training seems lacking in most organizations. In other words; you show which God you believe in by how you treat others.

During the dispute concerning Judaism's part in the continuance of Christianity, the Apostles told Paul to remember the poor, not to teach some important creed that must be emphasized concerning orthodox thinking. Taking care of the poor is an act of love, as you are helping those that cannot return the favor. This is the orthodox doctrine that all should pursue. Paul was considered the first theologian, as he explained many of the Christian concepts through his writings; careful reading and studying of his letters may enlighten you that he always was trying to get the body of Christ to show love in all their being. The so called chapter of love should be called the gospel chapter, because it speaks to us on how to act as Christians. The most important and hardest object to realize is love and can only be accomplished through the Spirit. In the Greek language there are many types of love, but with any act you can tell whether the act is selfish or real love, as real love is not for personal gain, be it reputation or material gain. Love that is shown by your actions is much more powerful than love that you feel.

ALERT SERVANT

Many people in probably every generation have proclaimed that the end of the world would come before most of them would die, as Jesus said his return would be like a man that leaves and puts servants in charge and they should be ready for his return. Everyone meets his or her eschatology in death, for there is no redemption afterwards. So for each one of us, in every generation, when we died, the world ends and then we will face the judgment. But religion will always claim to know more than what is found in the Bible and will also try to control the meaning of what it is to be Christian. The antireligious concept embedded in this short parable, or saying, is that religion does not have the answer.

Furthermore, although many create doctrines and other beliefs thought up by interpretations of the Bible, Jesus said that the prophets spoke about him. When you read the Bible, you should be looking for Jesus, so as to obtain eternal life. Eternal life does not come by believing or following some belief system made by human minds, no matter how far back the tradition goes, nor does eternal life come from ritualistic participation, but by trust and accepting what God is doing in your life to make you Christ-like. The other alternative is to follow creeds and dogmatic beliefs that are dry and dead and make the follower empty subjectively, because God's Spirit does not reside in systematic, organized organizations that claim to hold eternal life, nor in human-made concepts that seem to interpret the Bible to some advantage.

REPENT

Another of Jesus sayings implies all must repent. It doesn't matter how good or bad you are; you need to repent. The antireligious is easily understood in that just because you are religious and follow some code of ethics, you still must, like all others, repent. Many people feel that although they are sinners, they do not need to repent, as they are living a life before God, and trusting in Christ, but we must repent every day, as we are not glorified, for we continually fall short of what it means to be Christian. To repent every day means to turn from your self-centeredness and be outward-centered. Some confuse repentance to mean an emotional experience.

The fear of God is one step in righteousness and another is repentance. Of course there is no set pattern. Both of these work together in order to create within us Godly-righteousness. Before regeneration, our righteousness only consisted in self-righteousness, but after giving God our self-righteousness, we can be molded by the Spirit into true righteousness. Self-righteousness manifest itself in bad faith only when we believe it saves us, because the only righteousness that saves comes from the blood of Christ. Of course, one attribute of self-righteousness is thinking we are better than others. No wonder it is very difficult to open our eyes to our own self-righteousness. That is why so many human-made doctrines of holiness cause individuals to think they are so wonderful and better than others that do not follow their dress code, living standards and ritualistic observances. Self-righteousness is the foundation of doctrines that cause division. This is the trap the Pharisees fell into, and a snare that we easily fall into whether we admit we follow some ethical code or not. In the ground of our being is where we find pride and evil intent. Ethical codes cannot change this part of our being. We must let the Spirit of righteousness change us through the blood of Christ. We through organization have left out repentance and righteousness, replacing those concepts with creeds and worldviews.

Nietzsche was right when he wrote that humans invented morals to control the weak or something in that train of thought. But God puts ethical thoughts in our being, yet we change and pervert our moral truths. Nietzsche denies these God given morals. Nietzsche saw the perversion of moral thoughts as if these thoughts were the source of ethical existence. But true moral righteousness can only come from a leading of the Spirit. This first comes about by what is known as the conversion experience. Just as William James explained, that if everyone had this conversion experience the world would be a much better place. No matter how few or much of religious Christianity we follow after the conversion experience, the touch of true righteousness will always make us holier.

FIG TREE

The saying that refers to the fig tree is in every synoptic Gospel. This saying has been misunderstood by many and even used by people to proclaim some new revelation that has been figured out and they teach it as the truth. The fig tree does represent Israel, but not in modern times; Jesus was referring to those that stood before him. Jesus was telling them that the church would be born in their generation and that was one of the last day signs. Also, because of the religious leaders' teachings, people believed that Jesus would overthrow the nations and make Israel the world power; even after many were converted, the concept stayed with some in the church for a long time. The budding of the fig tree was its growth and this growth came about by the creation of the Church. The Church is the grafted-in limb that has a Jewish foundation and the reason we use the Bible. So we were grafted into the fig tree and need the fig tree for food.

CHILDREN IN THE MARKET

This saying is typical of all generations and every individual if you understand the Christian text existentially. The Bible can be understood in other ways besides existentially, but the meaning of the text does not change because of a point of view. The authors only meant to teach what was written, and not for us to create our own understandings. Because God does something significantly personal in each of our lives to prove that there is a loving creator, this something significant will make us realize that there is a creator that cares about our personal feelings; for God has felt our pain while he, as Jesus, walked on this earth and was slain without reason. Since we are all different, God works on each of us in many different ways in order for us to understand; therefore, this personal act of God makes us all without excuse.

It is human nature to rationalize these actions in order to keep in touch with the subjective self-centeredness. We, like those in Christian writings, rationalize that John the Baptist and Jesus had faults in order to deny the importance of God in our lives. We all do this even as we try to let the Spirit control our lives, as the desires of the flesh fight the will of the Spirit. But in our patience, we can win by letting the Spirit control our lives, thereby overcoming through God's power.

SHEEP AND GOATS

This saying is only recorded in one Gospel, but is frequently spoken of in churches; yet its implications are not realized by most. The question should be asked, why did those that helped not know that they had done good things, while those that didn't help thought they had done good things? The answer is simple because it has to do with our own being. If you do things because you think your actions are justifying you, you are mistaken. But when Spirit-controlled, you do things naturally, and you don't realize you are doing anything good; as the acts become your nature for, it is an expression of your being. The goats believed they were justified before God, while the sheep didn't understand why they were justified. Any one of us as a Christian can say that we have no idea how God can justify us as we are no better than anyone else, but God changes our hearts and we do those things that are good when it becomes part of our personality. We can look within ourselves where no one else can see and know that we are so far from what God would want us to be because of our shortcomings. We can see our own sins, yet truly cannot really see the sins of others.

On the other side, we can believe that we are so good or justified before God and even think that God has seen something within us to cause him to choose and change us then save us. We think that our good works is what God has for us to do as if it were our ministry; but we only fool ourselves into believing we are secure in our salvation. Our true works are self-centered and full of iniquity. We want to bring glory on ourselves even when doing well; we rationalize calling our actions the work of God. How easy is it to fool ourselves? We are all self-centered, for we believing what we think is correct and we are not able to see our iniquity, for our train of thought makes us feel important subjectively and gives us demonic confidence. Demonic means that our thoughts are tainted with more than the purity of being other-centered.

WISE SERVANT AND STEWARD

These sayings are much like the Alert Servant. Jesus would have probably told the same stories over and over again, changing the wording a little depending on his audiences. And even though the stories may be somewhat the same, each could have a different ethical meaning. Most of what Jesus said was not recorded, as it would have filled so many books that even the works written by the interpreters would be unreadable in our lifetime, and since Christianity is not suppose to be based on some Gnostic concepts or intellectual pursuit, more writings would have seemed to make knowledge more inherent for the belief system, and that is not Christianity. This is another reason why we need the Spirit in our lives instead of intellectual ill-rationalized interpretations. Knowledge is important, but without the Spirit, any type of thinking is absurd, vein and more than likely demonic.

The parables of the Ten Minas and Talents are much the same, with the same meaning behind them, as they both deal with the heart of the individuals that were given something that wasn't theirs. Each was told to invest it, but some hated the master and so would not work for him, because some still believed he was cruel. This is another illustration of parables that seem the same and yet are different, yet with maybe the same ethical impact. The antireligious view that we must change our hearts and not our religion is what guides most of the parables. But we cannot really change our hearts and must rely on faith in Christ to become Christ-like.

These stories are teaching us to watch our soul with patience, for many that start the walk end up with hardened hearts and forget to follow the fruit of the Spirit. Many have instead found comfort in dogmatic beliefs that only wound others instead of giving the life that is in the Spirit. In this way those that leave the Spirit for manmade dogma spiritually beat others and eventually become drunk on their own self-righteousness. These beatings are typical from many self-righteous church leaders. Not physical beatings, but spiritual beatings that do not lift up the Body of Christ even though leaders contend it produces righteousness. So the existential symbolic interpretation is both antireligious and shows the decline of the ethical. This acceptance has led the church to grow in the acceptance of sin. Sin is the norm, not the exception in our churches.

TWO DEBTORS

This saying is antireligious, as Jesus is telling Simon that he, Simon, could not love God more than those that Simon thought of as sinners. Even Simon confessed that according to his personal philosophy that he couldn't love God as much as those that he looked down on as sinners, for they had more reason to love than did Simon himself. That is contradictory to what Simon believed. His systematic philosophy easily fell apart before Jesus. Simon's belief and teachings accepted and announced that through God he was rich, for he had found favor in God's eyes. Those that were sick and poor were in this state due to their sins or sins in their family. Jesus was a contradiction to Simon, as Simon's philosophy was full of contradictions which were revealed in Jesus. Simon relied on his knowledge to save him, and knowledge can only lead you to salvation by following Christ. All other knowledge will be contradictory when not pointing to the self-existing one. No matter what type of knowledge you use or what kind of philosophy you understand life through, human concepts are only able to bring you to understanding the evil that is really in our hearts. Our hearts are self absorbed in what we believe is right and will always lead us to choose the wrong road, because our intentions are actually evil, no matter how righteous, kind or sympatric we find ourselves in any situation. So the story that Jesus told revealed this contradiction.

Just as there are consequences to our actions, there are also consequences to our thought process. So the ethical is encapsulated in the antireligious theme in that no matter what systematic belief we have, it will always contradict itself. We, like Simon, would contradict what we believe if we take our thoughts to their ultimate conclusions. This is what Jesus did to Simon while asking him the question about the parable. We say more in both the negative and positive than what we think as we talk, even though most of us just accept ideas, as we are shallow, not looking at the total concepts or the implications of what we say and think. Therefore, we are blind and our actions and thoughts may be against God's will. This is why Paul said that evil is always present even though he wished to do well.

LEAVEN AND THE MUSTARD SEED

Returning to these sayings is worth it, as there is a lot to learn from these short parables. Jesus spoke of the kingdom of God and that is a direct reference to the church. This was a problem, as the Bible teachers taught that the kingdom of God was going to happen when the Messiah came to overthrow the governmental powers that were suppressing the Jewish nation. So, by saying the kingdom of God was at hand, Jesus was proclaiming himself to be the Messiah. The religious leaders got it wrong again, just like those at the time of Noah, and you could rationalize that the religious leaders of today probably have it wrong to the point that many will miss the truth. This is the critical thinking that Jesus spoke about.

These sayings are very misunderstood as they are traditionally taught about someone's personal sin, when in fact both stories are talking about as the church grows, sin grows. The yeast is a type of sin that grows as the church body grows and the animals that fly and land on the mustard tree are false leaders that begin to control the church. There are three ways the church grows. One is by increasing its acceptance of sin. The second is excessive and powerful evangelizing, and the third is through persecution. Only the third seems to create a church that is perfect as individuals literally give their lives for Christ.

Church history is full of ups and downs, where sometimes the Church was very powerful and other times didn't look like she would survive. It is easy to criticize those in the past, but it is very hard to understand them, just as, if they were to resurrect today, they wouldn't understand the technology that we take for granted. But if we could give all of church history to the historians and use the parables as the basis for doctrine, the results would perhaps be a much more spiritual Church. Not through the writing of objective creeds that are found throughout church history, but through the subjective understanding of what is the Church. These two parables would teach us to watch ourselves and our leadership to make sure we are all following all that is holy. The heart of the Bible is the gospels, the heart of the gospels is the parables, the heart of the parables is the Church, and the heart of the Church is Jesus. The parables as well as the Bible at large all point to Jesus.

TWO SONS

We are the son that finally does what we are asked to do, or we are the son that believes we are good enough—even better than those that are not so blessed—and we believe we don't have to do anything for God's acceptance. This saying is another anti-religious saying, but it is not talking about the church, as the phrase *kingdom of God* is not used when telling the story. The son that said he would and then didn't is referring to the religious leaders that Jesus was talking to and by answering his question these religious leaders were condemning themselves. These religious leaders represent religious people throughout history and not just the Jewish teachers or followers of Judaism. Although the religious leaders probably knew the parable was about them, they more than likely didn't grasp the total intent of the lesson Jesus was trying to teach. They, like the son, deceived not only their followers, but also themselves into believing their actions were appropriate. Similarly, religion can blind us to the true meaning of what it means to be Christian.

The son that said, "No," but did what is right is typical of us that enter God's favor whom were once unacceptable and rebellious to God's authority. After the work of the Spirit changes us, we come to understand how important God is in our lives. We are the sinner and tax collector, a type of person at the bottom of the social ladder. It doesn't matter what standard of living you have or what religion you follow, you must repent or you will perish. All of us are under this condemnation and must do what God asks in order to be part of the next life. All that is in the world is vain and empty and cannot give us what God will give us in that great day. But we must understand that the church is as good as it is evil.

With change there is always stress and other factors, like depression. While God is changing us, we should not be amazed that we do not feel as if life is even worth living, even though we should be happy that God is working in us. But it is impossible for us to simply give up, as we now have the spirit that cries out to God for help. Our complete being has changed and it affects every one of us differently, but is a struggle that we must all go through as our subjective-self is slowly changed by God's Spirit. This change will last the rest of our lives until the day we die or are caught up to meet Jesus in the heavens. Therefore, we shouldn't be amazed that we are in such a struggle.

TREASURE AND PEARL

Those that claim that Christianity is ethnocentric because the Christian text states that Jesus is the only way do not understand what Christianity is or how to interpret that statement. All religions point to God in some way. Even those that are non-theistic or that even worship Satan point to the true Creator, for the Creator made Satan. All these religions give us a glimpse of what is God and that the human spirit was created to worship him. Someone that is seeking the truth may go through many more than one of these religions in a pilgrimage trying to satisfy the soul. Christianity would claim that all these belief systems fall short of God's full desire for all of us. Once finding God, true searchers will leave all other belief systems behind and believe that Christ is the only way.

Most people that point fingers at others shouting accusations of ethnocentricity are more than likely ethnocentric themselves. These people will point fingers at Christianity, but leave other belief systems that are one sided without judgment. The truth is they have a hatred focused at Christian beliefs because of their self-centeredness. These types of people are self-pleasing and really care nothing about social or religious life. They only want Christianity out of the way, as it teaches to put others first and this concept contradicts their meaning for existence.

These two sayings are referring to the church because of the use of the phrase, *kingdom of God*. They both have a simple meaning and that is when you find the truth of Christianity you will sell all you have and buy into what it means to be Christian. Once someone really becomes a Christian, they cannot find anything better. This is because Christianity becomes a relationship and not a religion. You will never lose the walk with God that is now a part of your being; even if you deny it, the power of the relationship will always remind you of what you are missing. God will forever contend with your spirit once you have understood the truth of Christianity.

SERVANT'S DUTY

This short parable has many important meanings and seems to be contradictory to the teachings that you don't have to do anything to stay saved. Well, maybe not quite if you look closely at the story. Just as the servant did what the master told him, Christians led by the Spirit, will do what is required. But we as servants should get no praise for just doing what we know is right by the Spirit. We should strive to know Christ more through our actions. Just as Jesus told the lawyers that they needed to do more than follow the law and pay tithes. They had forgotten another aspect of the law and that was to love others and to have mercy on those that needed help. To care about the needy that cannot help themselves or are in a bad situation is that part of the law the legalists forgot to follow. As a Christian, God gives you a nature that causes you to desire to follow his rules by being led through the Spirit. Many Christians are legalistic without realizing their belief system has developed thought legal systematic theology.

Following of the Spirit is our duty and we should not think we are better or that we should receive something special because of what we may be doing in Christ. Many people walk around with their humbleness puffed up because they think they walk in the Spirit, but humble obedience is our reasonable duty. Growing in Christ is also our duty; it is not something that we do to receive a better reward. When we reach the end of our lives, all we can say is that we did our duty. All that God has waiting for us is unearned; none of us deserve the blessings of God. We are evil, not God. Even giving up our lives is not a sacrifice that makes us any more worthy, because we are sinners and will die anyway and the wages of sin is death. It is amazing how so many of use act or believe in our hearts that we are more worthy than those that we know who go or don't go to church.

CHAPTER 9

SAYINGS CONTINUED

Most Christians salute the sovereignty of God but believe in the sovereignty of man.

R. C. Sproul

Why do you call me, 'Lord, Lord,' and do not do what I say?

Luke 6:46 (The Bible—New International Version)

EVERYONE IS GUILTY

Although it is easy to condemn the church using historical information, there are also good things that people have done in the name of the church. This is true today; the church building is where all types that confess to Christianity meet, creating an organization for the aid in helping others, as the Apostles told the Gentiles to remember the poor. Islam and Christianity have had a bloody, violent past, but we in the so-called Christian world forget about things our ancestors have done in the name of God. There has always been a battle between the spirit of prophecy and the spirit of organization within Christianity. But the Christ-like spirit is something other than either prophecy or organization. It is up to each of us to find this subjective spirit and thereby know God. There is no such thing as a Christian organization or a Christian nation. In this sense the history of Christianity is a myth.

If you don't question your beliefs, then you really don't believe what you affirm. What does this mean? This means that when you study, you should understand both sides of an argument and continually question those ideals and concepts that you have been taught and accepted. Studying and understanding a subject in depth is much better than being shallow and just accepting what is told you with the narrow interpretation you were taught. There are many anecdotes that were created by those that wish to understand the issue from only one side, but those stories will never bring us to the truth of a situation. To truly understand why someone believes the total opposite of what you believe brings you to a ground of understanding of yourself more than any discipline can reveal to you about the human condition.

Atheists are just as guilty of being one sided as Christians and other religious people. In fact, this seems to be a human condition. Those that follow atheisms have shed just as much blood, if not more, as anyone in the name of a religion has done in the past. No matter what we believe in our sect, we cannot point a finger at others as all history is just as tainted in anyone's organizational religious history. So, it is naive for an atheist to condemn religion and claim that religion is a human problem when wars and injustice would still be a part of the human experience even if religion were not only illegal but also completely wiped from human existence.

PHARISEE AND TAX COLLECTOR

This parable is easy to understand as the full explanation is almost given to the reader. The parable shows an antireligious thought in that the Pharisee's way of thinking was incorrect and the tax collector becomes the saintly one or good guy. This is the opposite of how people were taught in relationship to their social order, and that also reveals a latent paradox. A subjective paradox is an existential understanding, not what the audience believed was right and wrong. The ethical stands out as most of us have felt like we were the Pharisee at one time and then the tax collector another time. In this way we can also empathize both with the Pharisee and tax collector subjectively in our personal thoughts at the same instant.

Since tax collectors were mostly disliked and Pharisees honored, this story would stir up many emotions from the audience. Emotions from the audience would stir up as the people believed Jesus was a prophet; furthermore, some believed he was the Messiah. This prophet spoke to their hearts through this and other parables by helping them to question their social feelings. We also need to question our social beliefs as we can easily be drawn to mistaken conclusions by our prejudices. These prejudices are so grounded in our social norms that we may not even perceive them as such. That is why there is always more to a parable than its explanation.

UNJUST JUDGE

There are different meanings for the word faith. The faith that Christ taught is that faith causes you to trust in

God even though it doesn't seem as though God is fighting your battles. Many people claim they believe and even have faith in God but live their lives as if God does not exist. They neither talk to God nor consider how God wants others to be treated. Faith is found in the actions of an individual that reflects that individual's personality. Christian faith is something you become, not something you decide to believe.

The paradox of waiting for revenge and also loving your neighbor is a perplexing concept, but it can be understood in this way: while someone is alive, there is still time for them to change and come to God. By following this mindset you fulfill the faith that comes from God. Those that are without God will only receive what they have had on this earth, for after death there is no hope. Therefore, we should be mindful of the non-believer's end and taking this into consideration should be a factor in all of us, drawing us to forgive them for anything.

In answering prayers it has been said that *God either says yes, no or wait.* This concept is a catchall phrase and doesn't explain God's plans in our life. God works on our spirit if we are his children. So trials and problems will follow us through our life that is controlled by God, so that we can become Christ-like. If you do not have the type of life where God is working on you, you are not a child of God. Unconditional love is not letting your children do what they wish, but is the actions taken to ensure they grow to be productive in respect to emotional and physical support. Many people confuse life's trouble with God not caring, or that God is unable to do what needs done to lower the painful reality of existence towards his children. In most cases, the more trials, the more closely your walk with God is and will become as you continue to grow in grace.

GREAT PHYSICIAN

The problem with those that think like the Pharisees is that they don't realize they need God. They become somewhat narcissistic in their attitude about subject matters and their personal thoughts seem to them to be correct. They believe that they already have what is needed and that they are saved. They are confident in their belief system and their distortion of the intent of the Bible. Many Christians need Christ, but with their dogmatic views, they learn to live without fellowship with God and rely on other concepts that keep them complacent. If you believe you have your theology correct, then you need to reexamine your life.

HIDDEN TREASURE AND PEARL

Both these parables deal with ethnocentrism in the Church. Jesus being the only way and truth is what most non-acceptors question when they wish to denounce Christianity. But these stories show that every religion has something to offer and that we all must be religious beings, but when we find Christ we will leave all other religious beliefs behind to follow Jesus.

It is inherent in every belief system that the paradigm perceived is the truest. So any worldviews from atheism to polytheism have this ethnocentric quality. Even within Christian sects, we find those that believe everything they acknowledge is correct; while other saints are logically wrong. This is a definition of ethnocentrism. The fact that all belief systems have a latent ethnocentric view does not mean that the individual that follows a religious belief is ethnocentric, for ethnocentrism exists outside of religious belief systems. It is ethnocentric to call religion ethnocentric. Ethnocentrism is a human condition and is found in most of humanity, above all in intellectuals.

WISE AND FOOLISH BUILDER

The audience was amazed as Jesus spoke to them as if he were addressing each individual. The religious Jewish leaders taught them as a nation. To the nation of Israel the Bible was about the nation and not the individual, as it probably is today. So the interpretation of stories and other historical points would only be directed to those that were of the nation as a body, and not individuals as we Christians should understand the Bible today. Those that did not do what was correct in the sight of God were used as an example not to follow. This might have been missing from the Jewish teachings. From Genesis to Malachi every Christian, when reading, should be able to see Jesus. It is a great thing when a Christian can use these writings to show that Jesus is the Messiah. But the Jewish nation would understand the Bible directing them as a nation to do what is right in relation to God.

The texts concerning the teachings surrounding the builders stresses a personal subjective understanding of following God. The objective religious life is rejected as it only shows an outward following and not an inward connection with God. God desires to dwell within and change us, as we cannot change ourselves. We must rely on a relationship with God to remake us in Jesus' image. Not to have this relationship means that we are self-righteous and will not be of any value.

HOUSEHOLDER

The Kingdom of Heaven is a reference to the Church and so this interpretation is much different than what many have taught. This saying is in a context that infers the actualized life of the members of faith called the Church. The Church is not an organization or the rulers of an organization and not the leaders in the church. Here Jesus uses the phrase *'teacher of the law'* to refer to those that are the true leaders in the body of Christ. We know that both wheat and tares grow in the church and it is hard to distinguish the difference between who is a child of God and who is demonic.

So who are these leaders in the Church? They are the individuals that bring people into the body of Christ through their evangelizing. When they bring someone to a point of becoming a new follower of Christ, they bring both the new and old. No one that is converted becomes completely new; although this would be an ideal situation, it never happens. We call these people soul winners. Some may denounce that term claiming that only Jesus calls and saves us, yet no one should complain about calling those that bring others to following Christ, leaders.

Some have referred to the treasures as meaning the old and new covenants, but this is taking the content out of context, for Jesus never referred to the different covenants within this section of teachings. Nor does the phrase 'Kingdom of God' refer to both covenants. The new covenant is the fulfillment of Moses' covenant and not a replacement. But each parable is speaking about the human condition of the body of Christ. To understand the new covenant, you must first understand the Mosaic covenant. And to understand the Mosaic covenant is not to understand it as an old outdated covenant that Jesus abolished, for Jesus fulfilled the ceremonial covenant.

KING'S WAR PLAN

Here Jesus is explaining to the crowd that subjective reality is truth. In other words, *truth is subjective*. The concept of truth being subjective is claimed by all existential thinkers and is also stitched into the Bible. Jesus is teaching the crowd that the great commandment is important as they should love God with everything they can *will-to-be* and that he is God. So by following Jesus you are following God's plan. This is not a call to asceticism, as you cannot honor God with your objective life, but can only follow God with a subjective relationship.

VINE AND THE BRANCHES

This section of writings consists of an analogy that attacks Gnosticism at its roots by using the Gnostic context to contradict the words of Jesus. The vine and branches found in symbolic language bring the belief system of Gnosticism to a point where a Christian cannot accept any Gnostic worldview. There exist many different worldviews in relationship to Gnosticism, but the one concept shared by all claims that the evil physical universe exists because it was created by an evil God. The only thing that Jesus claimed was evil was you and I, due to our depravity. Depravity is a descriptive word, although not used until Augustine. We find the Gnostic views opposite of what God said in Creation, since everything God made was desirable. The same word translated 'good' in Creation is translated lustful in a different book in the Bible. Therefore, to the true Gnostic this type of God becomes contradictory to Jesus and the history of the Jews.

Wine was a very important part of society and was used for daily consumption and probably for medicinal reasons as well. By using this analogy, the Gnostic believer would have to realize that what they considered evil in the Gnostic's view; Jesus considered good. Wine could not be both evil and good. If wine is important, then the vine and branch must also be seen as important Therefore, if these physical items are good, then all matter must be good. Along with all the other attacks against the Gnostic's train of thought within this Christian text, the Gnostic Christian could see the errors and convert to a real relationship with Christ.

The most acute sin problem in the churches and organizations today in reference to Christian leaders is the refusal to accept questioning and debating the truth of doctrine and claiming that doing so is rebellious. With this viewpoint no one can question dogma, for by doing so it is the same as rebelling against the authority of the church organization and the leaders in the local assembly. But Paul said that those who studied to see if the teachings were correct were more honorable, as their relationship with Christ seemed important. This means they questioned everything, which may have a direct link to being under the Pharisee's teaching of not questioning authority.

The metaphor also carries a latent philosophy that we can do nothing without Christ, and when we are under God we will experience pruning in order to bring forth more fruit. This fruit is not evangelizing others, but a direct reference to the subjective-self becoming more Christ-like. This train of thought contradicts what Gnostics believed important. The important aspect for a Gnostic is some secret knowledge that one must understand in order to find salvation. Today false teachers call this a revelation that only true followers learn. For the Gnostic, Christ is no longer needed, as salvation comes through rejecting the physical world. But now through this text the Gnostic may understand a relationship makes us Christians, not knowledge.

Knowledge is the core of what it means to be Gnostic. Today we are not faced with Gnostic belief systems within Christianity, but most Christians have Gnostic tendencies that have been handed down through Catholicism. Also, many sects that claim to be the only true church do so by teaching that they have the correct knowledge for you to follow, and the other churches that do not follow this important information are in error, for God has not opened up their eyes to see the truth. This kind of understanding is more of a mystery cult than a Gnostic belief system but inherently has Gnostic tendencies.

BREAD OF LIFE

The first three writings of the canonized Christian texts are considered synoptic, as they have sections in common. The fourth book is Gnostic, but unlike other Gnostic writings, the didactic quality of this writing is that it takes Gnostic views and reveals the error of Gnosticism. So when considering what Jesus was trying to teach, we need to understand the didactic quality in the light of converting a Gnostic believer. Gnosticism existed before Christianity, and then a blend of both worldviews taught that believers needed more than just the blood of Christ to save them. The problem of adding some philosophical belief with grace has always been the backbone of error in theology. Also, most Gnostics taught that this salvation was what they had to do on their own.

The whole section examines the message that concerns this parable. Because many didn't understand what Jesus was saying, they quit following him. Although at that time there were no Gentiles following Jesus, Gentiles desired and still sought for some logical knowledge, while the Jews wanted signs from Jesus to prove he was the Messiah. Of course, as we read, we learn about many signs and wonders that Jesus did and the logic that he taught. It should amaze us that those that asked for signs and wanted wisdom did not accept what Jesus already had given them.

We have already addressed the issue of the wine, but now the focus on the bread becomes important. When Jesus proclaimed that the bread was his flesh, the audience couldn't understand that he was speaking figuratively. There are many examples in the Bible of the bread being a type of Christ, but the Jewish nation did not understand this as they were looking for a political Messiah and not exclusively a religious leader. It is difficult even today to divide the written word and know what are shadows and types of Jesus. Apparently, this type of figurative speech was missing from the teaching of the religious leaders of that time. This missing figurative example along with other traditions may be one reason many could not understand Jesus' proclamation of bread and wine.

Jesus had to correct their philosophy and explain that the bread from Moses was not from heaven, but that he was the bread from heaven. To believe on Jesus was what they needed to receive eternal life. The food that Jesus provided was not only a miracle, but also taught the Gnostic Christian that the God that is the Creator is not evil. Producing an abundance of leftovers from just a small amount of food would have been confusing to the Gnostic Christian, for all matter was evil. So by Jesus claiming to be the bread from heaven, the Gnostic Christian would have to reexamine his complete belief structure. Interpretations that leave behind the Gnostic way of believing change the true didactic meaning of the writer of this Gospel.

GOOD SHEPHERD

In the fourth Gospel there isn't as much anti-religion, as it is mostly anti-Gnostic. When reading this Gospel, it is best to remember what the Gnostics believed and interpret how the text would challenge their beliefs and force the Gnostic toward orthodoxy. Not that historical orthodoxy is always correct, but it can be understood as a standard. The purpose for this Gospel is to bring those Christians that are in error back to the right way of thinking. That is the purpose of all the Christian writings, so that Christians can know how to think. Unfortunately, there are many false teachers that want to take things out of context and there are many true saints that get carried away with their graceful teachings.

In the story of *The Good Shepherd,* we find many systematic teachings that speak to the Gnostic Christian. The first of these three steps is by telling the Gnostic reader that the children of God know what voice to follow. This claim is telling the Gnostic that they are carried away with Gnosticism; they are listening to the wrong voice. It is not some knowledge that they need in order to know God; to know God they must know the very voice of God. Those in Gnosticism are taught through these sayings what to believe, as a contradiction arises when listening to someone; as true orthodoxy teaches they should have been hearing the voice of God. The relevance today is that many traditional ways of Christian thinking have been influenced by Gnostic tendencies.

In the second step, Jesus begins to explain to them that he is the voice and that all other voices are thieves and killers. All other voices are there for their own personal rewards, but Jesus is there because he is taking care of his sheep. This creates an opinion that the Gnostic teachers are deceivers and out for themselves. The wording is an explanation of what Jesus was trying to tell them, but the audience didn't quite understand, so his explanation took a direct approach. This *idea of the audience not understanding is in all the Gospels* and is used for didactic reasons. While reading the accounts of what happened in the Gospels, we may say to ourselves, "why can't they get it, it is so simple?"

The third and last step is built on the other two steps. In it Jesus covers two dogmas that were wrong with the Gnostic's view. First, Gnostics believed that the creator was evil and second they didn't believe in a resurrection. Jesus built up this attack by saying he is one with the father, and in this proclaiming that the Creator is not evil. Then Jesus talks about being raised from the dead, for that pleases the father. This is an attack on those that do not believe in the resurrection. The very last thing that is emphasized is that Jesus is real because of the miracles that he has done. These miracles prove that he is from God. This concept is seen throughout the fourth Gospel as it further uses Gnostic language against Gnosticisms.

NEW WINE AND NEW CLOTH

These two sayings are much misunderstood when one tries to interpret them as a comparison between Judaism and Christianity. In no way was Jesus comparing the two different religions. This is absurd, as he sent those that were healed to the temple to perform the ritual given by Moses. Jesus would have never sent people to the temple if he was fighting against the corruption in the temple to the extent of denying any Jewish religious Biblical authority. To believe Jesus was against the totality of the Jewish teachings is not only incorrect, but also very anti-Semitic. Anyone that believes that these concepts are teaching anything about an old and new belief system is not only in error, but will pass on to other demonic concepts that probably originated for those cults that didn't support the nation of Israel.

These sayings are antireligious, as Jesus refers to other disciples that were not his, and their error in what was thought in respect to righteousness. These followers that were not Jesus' disciples were judging Jesus and his disciples according to their own opinion of what religion was, as Jesus contradicted almost everything they believed or may have been taught. The demonic behind all the questioning was that these other disciples were not asking for answers but were questioning Jesus' belief system in a rhetorical manner. A couple of times Jesus had to answer their questions even though it was only in their hearts and they gave no verbal comment. So these two sayings are referring to the difference between God's righteousness and the human condition of what is righteous. This was a condition of the heart and not a dichotomy between different belief systems.

CHAPTER 10
DOCTRINE

Woe to you, teachers of the law and Pharisees, you hypocrites! You give a tenth of your spices—mint, dill and cumin. But you have neglected the more important matters of the law—justice, mercy and faithfulness. You should have practiced the latter, without neglecting the former. [24]You blind guides! You strain out a gnat but swallow a camel.

Matthew23:23 (The Bible—New International Version)

Biblical orthodoxy without compassion is surely the ugliest thing in the world.

Francis Schaeffer

For a man to conquer himself is the first and noblest of all victories.

Plato (Dialogues: Phaedrus)

SACRAMENTS

What are sacraments? Many reformers have indicated their ideal list of sacraments, each with different ideas of what should be considered as sacred in the Church. But the Eucharist is a good example of how tradition and creeds are changed throughout history, then seen as literal interpretation of Christian text. Today many of the Christian sects use a piece of bread and wine or grape juice and repeat the words written by Paul, but history informs us that those that participated in the Lord's supper were socializing in more of a type of pot luck dinner. Wouldn't someone be startled if you told them you were bringing a roast to celebrate the Eucharist? The Lord's Supper has its roots in Judaism and not the Christian writings.

The problematic reality is that churches have divided over the use of wine or grape juice as if the argument was based on some Biblically correct interpretation and had some roots in salvation. This absurd disagreement has even gone as far as arguments as to whether the grape juice was fermented during the wedding the Jesus attended. Not much more should be written about these situations except that with such discussions still dividing Christians, it reveals the weakness of knowledge concerning the understanding of the didactic quality of the Bible.

EXISTENTIALISM VS. DECONSTRUCTIONISM

The phrase, *'in and of itself'* has no meaning. This is because *'no man is an island'*, for everything that exists is not exclusive and therefore anything is in relationship to every other thing. All things exist in relation to time and

189

space and may participate in "becoming-something" and "is-something" at the same time. Objects also have a relationship in a different form that we know as subjective knowing. To deconstruct anything tangible or intangible only distorts the existence of that something; just like taking a sentence out of context in order to make a certain viewpoint even though the author taught the opposite is a distortion proved through a deconstructionist. We are disconnected when we are not in a relationship with Christ.

The Bible is existential, for God is being, and can be understood by the words of King Solomon, carried through by the Apostle Paul, and then picked up by Kierkegaard and Tillich; the last two showed that true existentialism is Christianity. Other existentialisms are *demonic*, or tainted. King Solomon proclaimed that all things are vanity, but that it is also the duty of all humans to glorify God. Second, the Apostle Paul reflected this same concept when he wrote that his past knowledge meant nothing and that to know Christ was what is important and that others should follow Christ the same way as he did. Third, Kierkegaard wanted people to quit playing church, and to be real Christians subjectively in the complete spheres of their own existence. Tillich lastly proclaimed that whatever you considered most important in your life manifests itself as your God in reference to your ultimate concern, but the way for you to find fulfillment was having Christ as your ultimate concern.

Existentialism should be understood as an all-encompassing existence in relationship to the ground of being; that ground is the subjective self that is the deepest part of our being that we cannot change, such as anxiety, loneliness, finiteness, self-centeredness and other things within us that only God can change. These emotions are central to the core of existence and are the flower of our sins. This is what causes us to be self-centered instead of outward-centered. This self-centeredness is what brings forth sin and why we cry to God for help. It is impossible to overcome this self-centeredness and therefore Pelagianism is impossible.

ABORTION

Abortion is not a Christian doctrine and many people are confused about this subject. *Hermas the Shepard*, whose writings were used somewhat the same as the canonized Christian writings are considered today before the wide acceptance of the Gospels and Pauline letters, condemned abortion. Today abortion is the continuance of the pseudoscience of eugenics. Eugenics is now under the banner of population control, but people are still dying from starvation. Christianity should not be part of the political structure, but by example teach against such practices by supporting one another in love. This issue has led Christianity to become just a political block instead of a deep religious value.

This is not a debate between pro-choice and pro-life, but should be thought of as a contention between responsible and irresponsible individuals. This puts the light on the true subject while the use of choice and life do not really explain the existential situation. The Biblical worldview and its counter view are encapsulated in the abortion debate.

GODHEAD CONTROVERSY

Throughout Christian history there have been contentions concerning the Godhead and the relationship between Father, Son and Holy Spirit. This will never be resolved until we realize that God should be explained first through existence and then essence. God's ways are above our ways and we will never understand until knowledge isn't important. Many people have devised different ways of adding to salvation by faith in respect to the Godhead and all these have been through the concepts of a doctrine of essence. The reason why God cannot be divided is because God's essence is existence.

Many do not understand the link between the Godhead and salvation until they study the history of Christianity and find that the different views of what is needed for salvation are grace alone and grace with something else added. Docetism and Gnosticism are just two examples of the reference to the Godhead and salvation. Today's Unitarians do not understand that the doctrines of Monarchianism developed historically along side the doctrine of the Trinity. In fact, they both teach the same dogmatic view that the other side is heretical. This historical evolution of any Christian concept of the Godhead is built on essence and not existence. Therefore God should be considered as subject and not the object of worship in relationship to salvation.

There is no paradox in God's existence, but humanity lives in a state of paradox and therefore cannot understand the relationship between the Father, Son and Spirit. In the beginning of Christianity this relationship was not questioned, but as human questioning entered into Christianity the importance of the issue was elevated above the need for a relationship between the Church and God. Therefore dogmatic beliefs in the essence of the relationship between the Father, Son and Spirit were replaced with a relationship of the individual and how that individual fits into the body of Christ for the purpose of building up the Church. This created the link between salvation and the contention of the importance of understanding the Godhead. It should be noted that when dealing with heretical groups the Apostolic Fathers spoke of unity as the important issue.

ASSEMBLE

At the birth of the Church the fellowship existed in meeting from house to house and those of the new way shared all things. This became the Apostles doctrine and not some formula that came to be known through some systematic theology. Other Christian texts infer that the Assembly all lived or met in some home. Some of these homes in which Christians met may have represented a type of a small plantation within a city, as households could consist of slaves and other kinds of workers. Other meeting places may have represented some type of synagogue. The society may have been very different than what we experience today. Therefore the way Christians met was probably adapted to their culture.

Clement was a man ordained by the Apostles. His writings were considered for canonization by some. He taught a different governmental structure of the church, as did Ignatius, who wrote about a different understanding of the way the church gathered. Most noteworthy is the tradition that the church held many of its important meetings on Sunday. This was to preserve Saturday as the Jewish Holy Day, as the Jewish Christians continued to follow their father's traditions, even while they understood that the ceremonies symbolically taught God's will and pointed to Jesus Christ.

In modern days as well as in the first century, we find Christians not attending an assembly due to the corruption that resides in organized Christian religions. But this is a human condition and reflects the nature of society, for individuals are corrupt, not the organizations. Yet believers should meet and fellowship with like believers; we should all grow in unity. In the first century, the Apostle Paul had to fight many doctrines that divided beliefs. Still today there are churches that stress their thinking is most important even though they may call themselves interdenominational. They are inundated with belief systems that divide. Interdenominational is a statement of being that one is not judgmental about dogmatic views, yet even those that claim to be nonjudgmental still hold to a dogma that creates division, as this is a human condition. It is not the organization or the written dogmatic statement that is corrupt, but the way we use those traditions and creeds. Anyone that relies on traditional arguments to express their Christianity will end up with despotism as their savior, which is not unity. Some types of unity and divisions cause many to look negatively at the modern sects of Christianity.

The Church, referring to the body of believers, must have doctrines and a belief structure or individual believers will fall for any idea that seems ideal. Through history we can see many traditions and creeds develop. We can condemn these leaders for their human condition, but through existential analysis the problem of our own blindness can be seen. This is not the opening of our mind to our own faults, but the existential realization that we are just as faulty as the leaders we condemn. As humans failed God throughout history from the time of Adam until Christ, we the Church also come short of what it means to follow God. So how can anyone find salvation? This is why salvation comes by faith through grace.

MARRIAGE

God is probably against any type of divorce, as his nature is long-suffering in relationship to us and the fallen angels, but we as humans make many mistakes. The two reasons by which we justify divorce are unfaithfulness and abandonment. These two conditions can become blurred when considering all the situations and attitudes that cause a breakup. Divorce is not just an objective action, but starts out with subjective thoughts, and is a selfish act in at least one of the individuals.

Unfaithfulness is when your spouse cheats on you over and over again without stopping. Of course, if you are the one holding back those aspects of marriage that draw your spouse to commit adultery, you may be more guilty then your spouse. Many justify their divorce even though they were guilty of treating their spouse with contempt and showed no real love toward their significant other. This is where the line is blurred, as this is an act of abandonment. Israel has abandoned God many times, while God still acts in such a way to reconcile with them. This nature of God puts a heavy burden us that are contemplating divorce.

Abandonment is when an unbelieving spouse decides they want no part of Christianity or what their spouse has become since accepting Christ as savior. The problem is that abandonment can take place even if the individual stays in the household. Also, if a believer acts in such a way as to emotionally abandon an unbeliever, then that Christian is not really a believer. To manipulate others into believing you are innocent is probably the most well-known sinful trait accepted within the body of Christ.

Paul addresses both male and female differently in respect to their weakest issues in a marriage. He attacks the females by telling them to be submissive and to honor their spouse. This may be the hardest trait for women to actualize in relationship to a marriage. But on the backside of the situation, Paul finds males weakness by informing them they should give up their lives for their spouse. Men find enjoyment in objective things and to give up and put everything lower than their wife is almost subjectively impossible. So with this rationality it is hard to decide which partner is the most submissive in a marriage. Inherently the individual that walks nearest to God manifests the most love.

RELIGIOUS LANGUAGE

The most deceptive problem in Christianity is the religious language. Religious language is the social construct of religious society. An example would be Kierkegaard's *Christendom*. The way we act, think, and say we believe in order to find acceptance by the majority in the church social environment can be very deceptive, for we act as part of the pack. When it is unacceptable to question what is believed, the leadership and even the individuals who accept this type of system have a problem. To be a Christian is to have a subjective relationship with God that changes your spirit, because God is Spirit. Acceptance in a social system has saved no one, even though many of us feel subjectively comfortable in such environments.

Religious language is what cults use to keep their members in bondage. How can you tell if you are in a religious cult? If you feel as though if you leave the organization you will lose your soul or your 'life with God', then you are in a cult. If your sect is called a cult and you believe that all other Christian sects are cults, then you are in a cult. If you believe that only your organization understands the Bible correctly, then you are in a cult. If you have any type of physical or financial fears upon leaving an organization, then you are in a cult. If you feel as though only those that believe in your doctrine are real Christians, then you are in a cult. The total freedom to question the belief system is one of the most powerful evidences that you are not in a cult. The freedom to express your own views is also evidence that you are not in a cult, but in contrast a reliance on a doctrinal viewpoint in addition to a belief in Jesus as the Christ may be a sign that you are in a cult.

The occult is a different concept and deals with the mystical. Those things in the occult are not to be considered Christian, yet Christianity has mystical attributes. The difference is that in Christianity the mystical is not to be hidden, as it is in the occult. The occult likes to use the word metaphysical because it is beyond the natural, so it seems to fit the definition, but metaphysics is a main branch of philosophy and has a very different application. It is hard to determine whether mysticism in Christianity is acceptable. Christians should look at the historical examples in order to find a solution to some of the mystical aspects that should be accepted in the Christian lifestyle.

SIN IS NARCISSISM

The love of money is the foundation of all evil, therefore what money can buy for the self, manifested within us as self-centeredness, grows into a will-to-sin. This is encapsulated in narcissism. As all sin is conceived because of our narcissistic tendencies, money is just the medium of exchange to get what we desire, no matter what the cost to anyone, including ourselves. In order to have a love for money, you must first love yourself, and be willing to do anything for money. If you internalize this you will become a narcissist. We all have narcissistic tendencies and that is an obscure reason we all have sin. Any type of sin is conceived with our narcissistic tendencies, as we convince ourselves that it is better for us to get what we want. We believe that we deserve whatever we desire, even though it didn't come from God.

RATIONALISM VS IRRATIONALISM
REASON VS FAITH
FREE WILL VS PREDESTINATION
OBJECTIVE AND SUBJECTIVE TRUTH

If the Bible is the source for authority, then why do we contend and divide over these topics since those writers known as Apostolic Fathers never wrote intensely on these issues? The authors of the Bible often spoke of doctrine, but they never stated one verbatim. Those that knew and were ordained by the Apostles only claimed that their status was equal with their readers. They wrote letters to the churches they addressed. Many of these issues that divide Christians do not have their ground in the Bible, but other philosophies throughout human history.

The Objective truth is rational. Although it cannot prove the existence of God, it does show evidence of God's existence, and also declares the greatness of God. The subjective truth is irrational, but also declares the greatness of God, because it is grounded in the objective world. Yet we through subjective and irrational truth can understand that there exists more than that which is visible. Many of these different ways of expressing an understanding of God and the universe, such as free will and predestination, are a way of looking at the coin from different sides. Not only can each view be shown to be absurd, but each has been developed into systematic philosophies or theologies. Their common ground is in their ontological ground of evidence. This is something that we find hard to believe because of the yes/no factor within our rationalizing existence.

Works Cited

Aristotle. *Rhetoric.*

Bacon, F. *The Essays.* Oxford: Oxford University Press.

Berkeley, G. (1774, 2010). *Siris.* Dublin, London: Google Books.

Calaprice, A. (2005). *The New Quotable Einstein.* Princeton: Princeton University Press.

Dawkins, R. (Number 3, Vol. 21). Ignorance is No Crime. *Free Inquiry Magazine* .

James, W. *Essays: The Varieties of Religiious Expereince/ Pragmatism/ A Pluralistic Universe/ The Meaning of Truth/ Some Problems of Philosophy.* Library of America.

Kierkegaard, S. (1956). *Purity of Heart.* New York: Harper & Row.

Locke, J. (1937). *A Letter Concerning Toleration.* Chicago: Century Co.

Martin Luther King, J. (1963). *Strength to Love.* Martin Luther King, Jr.

Plato. *Dialogues: Phaedrus.*

Plato. (2010). *The Last Days of Socrates.* Classic Books International.

The Bible—New International Version. Biblegateway.com.

Tillich, P. (1958, June 14). The Lost Dimension In Religion. *The Saturday Evening Post* .

Voltaire. (1752). *"Catalogue pour la plupart des écrivains français qui ont paru dans Le Siècle de Louis XIV, pour servir à l'histoire littéraire de ce temps," Le Siècle de Louis XIV* . Paris.

[1] The Lost Dimension in Religion
[2] "Essays"

Manufactured By: RR Donnelley
Breinigsville, PA USA
January, 2011